THE GREAT BRITISH
BAKE OFF

HOW TO AVOID A
SOGGY
BOTTOM

AND OTHER SECRETS TO
ACHIEVING A GOOD BAKE

GERARD BAKER

BBC
BOOKS

10 9 8 7 6 5 4 3 2 1

Published in 2013 by BBC Books, an imprint of Ebury Publishing.
A Random House Group Company.

Text © Love Productions 2013
Illustrations by Tom Hovey © Woodlands Books Ltd 2013

Gerard Baker has asserted his right to be identified as the author of this Work
in accordance with the Copyright, Designs and Patents Act 1988

The Random House Group Limited Reg. No. 954009

Addresses for companies within the Random House Group can be found at
www.randomhouse.co.uk

A CIP catalogue record for this book is available from the British Library.

ISBN: 978 1 849 90589 3

The Random House Group Limited supports the Forest Stewardship Council® (FSC®),
the leading international forest-certification organisation. Our books carrying the FSC
label are printed on FSC®-certified paper. FSC is the only forest-certification
scheme supported by the leading environmental organisations, including Greenpeace.
Our paper procurement policy can be found at www.randomhouse.co.uk/environment

Commissioning Editor: Muna Reyal
Project Editor: Laura Higginson
Editors: Imogen Fortes, Lindsay Davies and Norma Macmillan
Editorial Consultant: Linda Collister
Production: Helen Everson
Design and typesetting: Smith & Gilmour
Illustrations: Tom Hovey

Printed and bound in the UK by Butler, Tanner and Dennis Ltd

To buy books by your favourite authors and register for offers
visit www.randomhouse.co.uk

THE GREAT BRITISH
BAKE OFF

HOW TO AVOID A
SOGGY
BOTTOM

AND OTHER SECRETS TO
ACHIEVING A GOOD BAKE

CONTENTS

INTRODUCTION

Whether you are already an avid baker wanting to improve your skills or just thinking about making a cake for the first time and interested to find out more, this book is for you.

How to Avoid a Soggy Bottom is not your usual cookery book, however. It's a helpful guide and a friendly companion to your well-stocked cookbook collection. By gently guiding you through the rules of baking, it will show you how to improve your techniques and hopefully give you the confidence to experiment with your own recipes or adapt recipes from your favourite books. Ultimately, it's going to make your baking better.

Every good baker should have a thorough knowledge of the art, science and history of their craft because learning about the origins of the processes and the principles behind them will really help you to understand why you do things a certain way or why things might not have worked. With this in mind, this book investigates the chemistry as well as the history behind the age-old methods we use – why baking powder was invented and how it works; how brewing came to play such an important role in breadmaking; why you cream a sponge cake, but use the rubbing-in method to make scones; and how gluten affects the texture of your pastry.

To help you along the way, there are tried-and-tested recipes that use the key skills explained in each chapter. Have a go at making yeasted and creamed sponge cakes, kneaded and unkneaded loaves, and rich pastries made with butter, olive oil and lard to see what they do to the bake's flavour and texture. These recipes will give you a good foundation to build on so that you can take your baking to new heights.

With this book in one hand and your wooden spoon in the other, you needn't fear the risk of over-whisked egg whites, damp biscuits, grainy caramel or, indeed, a soggy bottom ever again.

Gerard Baker

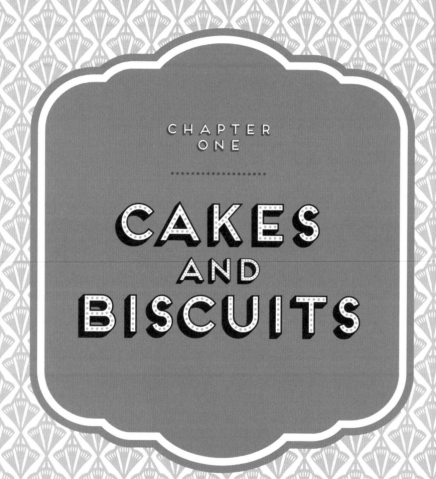

CAKES
AND
BISCUITS

Cake-making is actually incredibly straightforward. By combining basic ingredients – flour, eggs, sugar and fat – you can create an astounding number of very different cakes. So why do we see such varying results, some intentional and some less so?

One explanation is the way in which the ingredients are combined. The techniques you use when you cream, rub in or whisk your cake mixture will all influence the outcome of your bake. How heat reacts with the different ingredients will also affect whether your cake is baked through, has risen correctly and has the light and airy or dense, sticky texture you were hoping for. Understanding these techniques and the principles behind them will therefore help you to ensure you get the result you want every time.

The differences between biscuits, cakes and breads were not clearly defined for many centuries, as we made biscuit-like breads and bread-like cakes, but slowly our knowledge of cake- and biscuit-making has evolved until they have become distinct crafts. From the search for a practical raising agent to replace yeast, to the introduction of eggs to create an airy sponge and the use of cookie dough to test an oven's temperature, baking has always adapted as we continue to invent ever-more ingenious techniques and ideas.

CAKES

·················

A SLICE OF HISTORY

 Where does 'cake' come from?

While the Greeks and Romans of southern Europe can be credited as the inventors of early cakes, the word 'cake' actually comes from northern Europe, and from the Old Norse word *kaka*, first seen in texts in the thirteenth century. (Both the English word 'cake' and the German equivalent, *kuchen*, derive from this Old Norse word.) However, *kaka* was nothing like what we understand by the word 'cake' today – in fact, it described a rough, round, dry, biscuit-like bread (oatcakes being one of the best surviving examples).

 What were early cakes like?

While the early inhabitants of northern Europe made biscuit-breads, it was the clever Romans and Greeks who learned to bake more doughy, sweet bakes using yeast mixed with coarse flour and sweetened with dried fruits or honey. These early cakes must have been dense and heavy with a strong yeasty tang – much more like today's breads than cake.

 ## From *kaka* to *kuchen* to the Victoria sandwich: how did we arrive at our modern-day 'cake'?

It wasn't until the fifteenth century that the texture of cakes became anything like the light, spongy varieties we enjoy today. Little, airy delicacies, such as sponge fingers and biscuits began to appear, but rather than using yeast to make them rise, these lighter cakes were made with eggs, beaten by hand for up to an hour and sweetened with the exotic delicacy of sugar. However, as eggs were not readily available, these tasty morsels were considered a luxury and enjoyed only by the privileged few. Eggs would not become common in cake baking until the eighteenth century and then gradually became the raising agent of choice until the invention of baking powder (for more on raising agents and eggs, see pages 28 and 32).

As baking techniques developed, the muddled evolution of breads, pastries, cakes and biscuits continued and the differences between the four types was often hard to define. This conundrum is perhaps most evident in some of our favourite regional cakes. Welsh Bara Brith (see page 12) is a good example of an early bread-like cake; Eccles cakes and Banbury cakes are more like pastry than cakes; while the flat, round Goosnargh cakes (similar to shortbread) might now be described more accurately as biscuits.

Finally, it was the cake-loving Victorians whom we must thank for giving Britain one of its most cherished and most baked cakes, the Victoria sandwich. The classic recipe for the jam-filled sponge was laid out by Mrs Beeton in her *Book of Household Management* in 1861 and has been proudly served at afternoon teas, school fêtes and bake sales ever since.

• •

BARA BRITH

Bara Brith (meaning 'speckled bread') is a fruity teatime snack and perhaps one of the best examples of a sweet bread-like 'cake' raised using yeast. Debates still abound in Wales as to whether it should be classed as a bread or a cake, and some modern recipes now omit the yeast and use self-raising flour, but the recipe below, which does contain yeast, remains true to tradition.

Makes 1 x 1kg loaf
10g fresh yeast or 5g dried yeast or 5g fast-action
dried yeast
160ml warm milk
45g soft dark brown sugar
340g strong plain flour

½ teaspoon fine salt
65g unsalted butter at room temperature
140g mixed dried fruit
25g chopped mixed peel
½ teaspoon mixed spice

1 x 1kg loaf tin, greased with butter

✻ If using fresh or dried yeast, place it in a small bowl and add half the milk. Mix together with a pinch of the sugar, then leave to one side for 10 minutes to begin reacting (it will look frothy).

✻ In a large bowl, mix the remaining sugar with the flour, salt and butter. (If using fast-action dried yeast add it to the dry ingredients now.) Rub the butter into the dry ingredients, then mix in the yeast-milk mixture (if using) and the milk. Knead the dough well for 10 minutes until it is soft but glossy and elastic.

✻ On a lightly floured worktop, spread out the dough into a flat, even layer approximately 2cm thick. Scatter the fruit, peel and spice evenly over the dough, then fold up. Knead the dough for 1–2 minutes to distribute the fruit fully.

✻ Place the dough in a large clean bowl and cover it with a damp cloth. Leave in a warm, but not hot, place for 1½ hours until doubled in size.

✻ To shape the dough, tip it onto the worktop and knead for 1–2 minutes. Roll the dough into a cylinder with a crease on the bottom and place in the greased tin. Cover with a damp tea towel and leave to rise until doubled in size.

❄ Preheat the oven to 200°C/400°F/gas 6. Glaze the loaf with a little milk, then bake for 25 minutes. Turn the oven down to 160°C/325°F/gas 3 and continue baking for 15–20 minutes. The loaf is ready when it is well browned and it sounds hollow when tapped on the base (or see page 43 for other ways to check it's baked through). Leave it in the tin for 5–10 minutes before transferring to a wire rack. Eat spread with butter and honey.

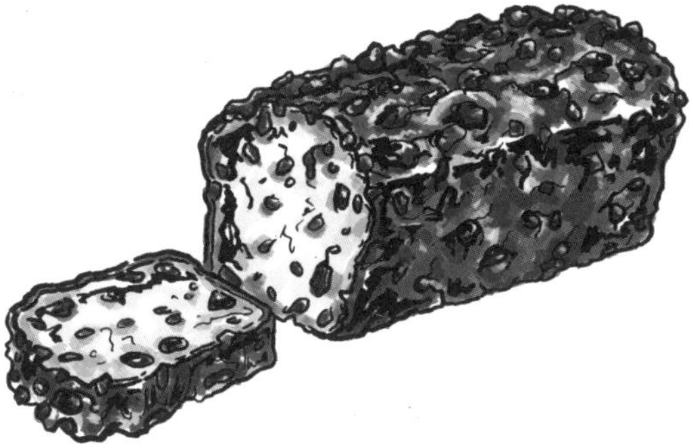

TYPES OF CAKE

 What is a sponge cake?

Light in texture with a tender crumb, a sponge cake – as its name suggests – has a light and 'holey' texture that will spring back when gently pressed. A sponge is made by whisking eggs with sugar and then mixing in flour. Some sponges may contain a form of fat too, but this is an optional addition. What is most essential is the amount of air created in the mixture, which is what gives it a light texture. There are three methods for achieving a good, spongy crumb: whisking, creaming and the all-in-one method (see pages 25 and 26). The Victoria sandwich (which does contain fat) is the best-known modern example of a simple sponge cake and can be made using either the creaming or the all-in-one method.

 What is a pound cake?

A pound cake is a version of the recipe used to make a creamed Victoria sandwich, but it uses equal weights – traditionally, one pound each – of butter, sugar, eggs and flour (self-raising flour nowadays). It is baked as a large cake and as 1lb equals 454g, a proper pound cake would weigh 4lbs, or a whopping 2kg.

The weights of the butter, sugar and flour are normally based on the ratio of one egg for every 50g of butter used. But as we all know, eggs vary considerably in size, and even if cookery writers give notes at the beginning of a book to specify the size of eggs to use, two medium eggs might weigh different amounts. Because of this, professional bakers measure eggs by weight, so that the recipe can be reproduced identically every time it is made. You'll see that in the recipe below, the quantities of butter, sugar and flour are based on the weight of the eggs removed from their shells.

A MODERN POUND CAKE

A true pound cake would require a very big round tin – 30cm or larger. This recipe makes a smaller version that can be baked either as one large cake, or in two shallower layers that can be sandwiched together with buttercream or jam. There are lots of ways to vary the basic cake (see page 18). Make sure that your ingredients are all at room temperature before you begin.

Makes 1 large cake or a sandwich cake
3 medium eggs at room temperature
unsalted butter at warm room temperature
caster sugar
self-raising flour
pinch of salt (optional)

1 x 18cm round, deep cake tin, or 2 x 18cm sandwich tins, greased with butter and lined with baking paper

❋ Preheat the oven to 180°C/350°F/gas 4. Crack the eggs into a bowl and weigh them. Measure equal weights of butter, sugar and flour.

❋ Set a large bowl on a cloth on the worktop (the cloth will stop it slipping). Put the butter in the bowl and beat it with a clean wooden spoon or hand-held electric mixer until it is soft, light and fluffy. Add the caster sugar and cream the sugar and butter together until the mixture is once again light and fluffy.

❋ Beat the eggs well with a fork to break them up. Add in small portions to the butter and sugar mixture, beating well after each addition until the mixture is light and glossy. When you have added three-quarters of the egg, make the next additions much smaller, to avoid breaking the emulsion between the butter and egg. (If this happens, the finished cake won't rise as well.) Once you have beaten in the last of the egg, sift in the flour. Using a large metal spoon, carefully fold in the flour until the mixture is even and there are no lumps.

❋ Transfer the mixture to the cake tin and smooth the surface gently with a spatula or palette knife. Make a small depression in the middle of the cake to help prevent the cake from doming in the centre during baking.

❋ Place in the centre of the oven. If you are making one large cake, bake for 20 minutes, then turn the heat down to 150°C/300°F/gas 2 and bake for a further 35–40 minutes. If you are making two small cakes, bake them for 20–25 minutes.

❄ The cake is ready when it feels firm to a light touch. Transfer the cake, still in the tin, to a wire rack and cool for 5 minutes or so before turning out (this helps prevent the cake from sticking).

For a vanilla-flavoured cake:
Add the seeds scraped from 1 vanilla pod to the creamed butter and sugar mixture.

For a chocolate cake:
Replace one-fifth the weight of flour with cocoa powder, and sift this with the remaining flour before folding into the cake.

For a coffee cake:
Dissolve 2 teaspoons instant coffee powder in 1 teaspoon hot water and cool; add this with the eggs.

For a lemon cake:
Finely grate the zest from 2 unwaxed lemons and add to the butter before creaming.

For an almond and cherry cake:
Add 25g ground almonds per egg, and the same weight of glacé cherries as eggs. Rinse and dry the cherries, then dust with flour before adding to the cake after you have folded in the flour and ground almonds. Add an optional ½ teaspoon pure almond essence to the eggs before

beating. Sprinkle the cake with 50g flaked or nibbed almonds and 1 tablespoon demerara sugar before baking.

For a seed cake:
Add 1 teaspoon caraway seeds with sugar.

You can also use this mixture to make fairy cakes using a 12-hole fairy cake tin, lined with cases. They will take much less time to bake, so watch carefully and remove from the oven when golden, risen and firm to the touch.

••

 ## Are fairy cakes and cupcakes the same thing?

The fairy cake is so-named because it is a tiny, light cake – suitable for fairies or, more likely, small children to enjoy. It is difficult to identify who first made fairy cakes and when (recipes like these crop up in kitchens across the country), but we do know that small cakes or buns have been baked for hundreds of years. The origins of these little, single-portion cakes are owing to the nature of early ovens. For although these days we might think nothing of switching on the oven to bake a cake or a batch of buns, two or three generations ago people had to plan their baking sessions a bit more carefully. When ovens were heated with wood, bakers had to bake according to its temperature, which would vary from when the fire was first lit to when it was cooling down.

Thus, cooks made bakes of different sizes: a batch of mixture was divided into one large loaf and a variety of miniature cakes or buns. The smaller bakes could be cooked in the hot oven before the larger ones went in to cook in the cooler, slower oven. These smaller cakes were therefore easier to make, compared to the larger versions that needed not only more time to bake, but also more skill when managing the fire.

We also don't know exactly when the name 'fairycakes' was first used. However, many recipes were developed after the Second World War by writers employed by cooker manufacturers to show off their equipment, and so-called fairy cakes appeared regularly in these compilations. Once again, the popularity of these little cakes was influenced by the technology of the ovens used to cook them. Traditional post-war fairy cakes are rather plain (and economical) – only a little glacé icing or buttercream would have been added to fairy cakes if you were lucky and could afford the added cost.

The name 'cupcakes' may historically come from the small, cheap earthenware cups or pots in which simple cakes were once baked. Amelia Simmons's pioneering book *American Cookery*, published in 1796, mentions little cakes baked in such 'cups', and in 1806 British cook Maria Rundell published a recipe in which her cake was measured using teacups. The other possibility is that the name comes from the use of measuring cups in American baking recipes. While fairy cakes are made using a basic pound cake recipe (see page 15), cupcakes are more frequently made using a higher proportion of flour and liquid and less fat. They have a drier texture and a finer crumb, which is why they're often topped with lashings of icing.

 ## What is a fruit cake?

A fruit cake is a typically British rich, heavy cake, made using the creaming method, in which at least half the weight of the cake is made up of dried fruit (including raisins, sultanas, glacé cherries and candied peel). Fruit cakes are associated with celebrations – they form the basis of wedding cakes and Christmas cakes and are often heavily decorated with marzipan and a rich icing.

Lighter versions of fruit cakes do exist: Madeira cakes are often baked with cherries in the mixture; and both Genoa and Dundee cakes contain a smaller ratio of fruit to batter than rich fruit cakes.

 ## When did we start to use fruit and spices in our cakes?

The fruit cake is unlikely to have appeared before the Middle Ages as it was only during the thirteenth century that fruit, nuts and spices arrived in Britain and subsequently appeared in our baking. Early medieval versions of the fruit cake can be traced back to Scotland – the 'black bun' was a rich fruit cake baked on special occasions.

Why do you boil the ingredients in some fruit cake recipes?

The method of boiling then cooling dried fruit before adding it to the dry ingredients is used as a means of making moist fruit cakes with a lower fat content. As well as containing less fat in proportion to the other ingredients, they also often contain as little as a quarter of the amount of flour normally used in a cake and the result is a tender, soft crumb.

The liquid you use to plump the fruit can vary from water or tea, to ale or even whisky or cherry brandy (which is particularly good) in more luxurious recipes – whatever you fancy.

BOILED FRUIT CAKE

Makes 1 cake
75g raisins
25g currants
25g mixed chopped peel
50g glacé cherries
75g unsalted butter
40g Muscovado sugar
300ml water or other liquid (see note opposite)
300g plain flour
1 teaspoon mixed spice
1 scant teaspoon bicarbonate of soda

1 x 20cm round, deep cake tin, greased with butter and lined with baking paper

❆ Combine the fruit, butter, sugar and water or other liquid in a heavy saucepan. Set over a medium-high heat and allow the mixture to come to a simmer, then reduce the heat and leave to cook gently for 5 minutes. Remove from the heat and pour the mixture into a large mixing bowl. Allow the mixture to cool until it is hand hot – no more than 40°C/105°F.

❆ Preheat the oven to 180°C/350°F/gas 4.

❆ Sift the flour, spice and bicarbonate of soda together into a separate bowl, mix in to the fruit mixture and transfer to the cake tin. Bake for 1½ hours until well risen and a skewer inserted into the centre comes out clean. Cool in the tin and transfer to an airtight box only when completely cold. Eat within two weeks.

••

CAKES AND BISCUITS

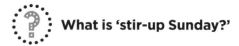

What is 'stir-up Sunday?'

This is an important day for many bakers! In the British Christian calendar the term refers to the last Sunday before Advent, the day on which Christmas preparations begin in earnest. Although the phrase 'stir up' derives from the opening phrase from the 'Collect' in the 1549 edition of the Book of Common Prayer that calls people to worship, in the kitchen, the phrase has come to describe the preparations of our Christmas mincemeat, pudding and cake.

The bittersweet dried fruit and alcohol used in modern Christmas cakes benefit from being given time to mature once baked so that the flavours become more rounded, and subtle. Because of this, stir-up Sunday might in fact be too late a date for a cake to have time to develop – a well-wrapped cake will keep easily for two or three months, and can be fed with alcohol throughout that time.

If you do choose to make your cake earlier in the year, make sure that you keep it in an airtight tin and in a cool place otherwise it might dry out or absorb flavours from other foods stored nearby. If you begin in October, you can then add a couple of tablespoons of rum each week up to December, then stop and allow the cake to mature before decorating it on Christmas Eve.

Don't be tempted to cut corners with the quality of any booze you put into your cake. Remember, it will only taste as good as the cheapest ingredient!

CAKE-MAKING METHODS

 Why are there different methods of combining a cake's ingredients?

Most cakes are essentially made up of four base ingredients: flour, fat, sugar and eggs. They are used in different proportions, but what changes the texture and consistency of the cake is the ratio of fat to flour and the method used to combine the ingredients. There are five main methods of making a cake: creaming, whisking, the 'all-in-one' method, rubbing in and melting. Find out below how and why each is used to create different results.

 What is the 'all-in-one' method?

The all-in-one method is the simplest way to make a cake. It involves less time and effort for the baker than creaming, but because no air has been incorporated in the mixture, the texture of the cake will not feel as light and the crumb will not be as fine or close. All the ingredients are put into a bowl and beaten with a wooden spoon or electric whisk until they are just mixed. You shouldn't beat the mixture much because if you did the gluten contained in the flour would be activated (see page 65) and the cake would end up tough. A little extra baking powder will compensate for the lack of air in mixtures using this

CAKES AND BISCUITS

method, and therefore ensures the cake rises, but don't overdo it or your cake will be dry. The all-in-one method is the easiest for beginners as there is less risk of the cake sinking in the middle.

 ## What is the 'creaming' method?

Creaming is also used to make sponge cakes which contain fat, and involves beating softened butter or other type of fat to incorporate air, lightening it both in texture and in colour (because the air beaten into the butter reflects light). The creamed butter is then beaten thoroughly with sugar, usually caster, which adds even more air through the mixture. Once the butter and sugar mixture is light and fluffy, the eggs are beaten in gradually. This is crucial; the eggs must be added slowly so that the emulsion between the fat, sugar and egg is maintained. The mixture will continue to absorb air as the eggs are beaten in.

When the eggs are completely incorporated, the flour is carefully folded in. Do this gently to avoid breaking too many of the air bubbles created in the mix.

 ## What is the whisking method?

The whisking method is used to make sponge cakes that contain little or no fat, such as Swiss rolls, roulades and Genoese sponges. The sugar is whisked with the eggs to incorporate plenty of air, which will give these cakes a very light spongy texture. The key is to make sure the mixture is very thick and pale before adding the remaining ingredients. (See also the recipe for a flourless whisked chocolate sponge on page 209.)

What are the rubbing-in and melting methods?

These are two alternative ways of making cakes that are used to combine slightly different proportions and types of fat, flour and sugar from those used in the all-in-one and creaming methods.

Mixtures that have been rubbed in tend to be dense and bread-like, such as rock cakes or scones (see also page 100). They have about half the proportion of fat to flour than a creamed sponge cake.

During the rubbing-in method, the fat is literally rubbed into the flour using fingertips, creating a fine crumb-like texture, before adding sugar and liquid. By doing this, you are less likely to overwork the gluten in the flour (see page 65 for more on gluten in flour), avoiding a tough finished cake and giving instead a crumbly but soft texture.

The melting method is used for moist, sticky cakes, such as gingerbread or parkin. It is the best way of dealing with ingredients that are difficult to combine at room temperature, such as honey, syrups and treacle. These ingredients are heated with the fat over a low heat before adding the dry ingredients.

GIVING RISE
TO YOUR CAKE

 ## When was baking powder first used?

After yeast and eggs, baking powder arrived as a means of making a cake rise. We have the Americans to thank for inspiring its invention, as well as for the 'self-raising' flours that incorporate it. Both have been around for only the last couple of hundred years; the first writer to mention powders rather than yeast for cake-making was Amelia Simmons in her book *American Cookery*, published in 1796, which also happened to be the first recipe book to appear from that country.

The invention of baking powder came about as a response to a particular problem faced by early American bakers. At that time, the yeast used to leaven bread dough (ale barm, see page 71) often turned acidic as it aged and produced heavy bread with a strong flavour.

Turning to chemistry, these ingenious eighteenth-century bakers realised that if they added an alkaline substance to the dough it would neutralize the acid. When an alkali was added to bread dough, these bakers also noticed that a gas was released (carbon dioxide) and the bread became lighter and tasted better. The first alkali used was the primitive pearlash, which derived from wood ash, then as the baking industry developed worldwide, many different compounds were used as an alternative.

Later, during the 1850s, two New York bakers, John Dwight and Austin Church, marketed another alkali, bicarbonate of soda, as a raising agent. They were the first people to produce it on an industrial scale, revolutionising both domestic and professional baking.

Today, baking powder usually combines bicarbonate of soda (an alkali) with cream of tartar (an acid) and a filler, usually corn or potato flour, which absorbs any moisture that might otherwise cause the two active ingredients to react together and render the powder useless.

Baking powders can contain several different chemicals. The next time you buy baking powder, check the label. Those powders that include aluminium compounds can give a cake or biscuit a metallic aftertaste – a good reason to avoid them.

 ## How can I tell if my baking powder is still active?

Baking powder can degrade in the cupboard, especially if it is not sealed in an airtight container because, if it comes into contact with any moisture, the active ingredients will react to produce carbon dioxide. Even if the level of moisture present in the air is small, the powder will react without you noticing, and when you next try to use it, it will fail you. To test if your baking powder is still active, add a teaspoon to a glass of warm water. You should see it quickly produce bubbles and become frothy. If it does not, it's gone off and you should replace it.

 ## Can I make my own baking powder?

It's easy to do this, but mix only as much as you need for the recipe in hand to keep it fresh. Thoroughly mix 1 teaspoon (5g) of bicarbonate of soda with 2 teaspoons (10g) of cream of tartar and use immediately.

 ## Can I make my own self-raising flour?

You know you should check your ingredients before you start baking, but somehow you just don't get round to it and suddenly you realise … the cupboard is bare! Even if you do have some self-raising flour, check its 'use-by' date; if the flour has passed it, its raising agents will no longer be active so reject it and buy fresh. Otherwise, if you can't get to the shops, why not make your own?

As a rule of thumb, 1 teaspoon (5g) of baking powder will raise 110g of plain flour, but baking powder packets give a handy guide to how much to use for each recipe. Make sure that the two are mixed well before you add them to other ingredients or your bake will rise unevenly.

Why do some recipes call for bicarbonate of soda or cream of tartar instead of baking powder?

Bicarbonate of soda and cream of tartar sometimes appear in recipes on their own. This is because ingredients such as fruit, honey and treacle are acidic in nature so they react with the alkaline bicarbonate of soda by themselves. This releases carbon dioxide into the mixture and has the effect of leavening the batter just as if you had used baking powder (which is a mix of acid and alkali, see also page 28). Cream of tartar is used mainly on its own in recipes where egg whites provide volume or lift. The acidic cream of tartar helps to stabilize the egg whites and make them more voluminous.

 ## Is baking powder gluten-free?

Some are and are sold as such, so you should check the label if you want to avoid gluten. If they are not labelled 'gluten-free', it is best to assume that they contain gluten because it can be present in the type of filler used.

ALL ABOUT EGGS

 Is it important to use fresh eggs for baking?

Eggs don't actually need to be very fresh to bake with. In fact, older eggs are easier to beat because they are more liquid.

To find out how fresh your eggs are, you can test them. If you crack a very fresh egg onto a flat plate, the yolk will stand proud from the white and you will see that the white consists of a firm circle of material with only a little clear liquid white surrounding it. Crack an older egg and you will see that the yolk is much less pert, and the white is very liquid.

If you store your eggs in the fridge, make sure you bring them back to room temperature before you use them for baking to prevent your cake mixture curdling (see page 45).

 Can I freeze eggs?

Yes, you can. Not whole in their shells, though! The best way to freeze eggs for later use is first to beat them well with a small pinch of salt (this helps break down the eggs) and pour them into an airtight container. Freeze them in multiples of two or four so that you can defrost just what you need for a particular recipe.

Defrost the eggs before using them: the best way to do this is to leave them in your fridge overnight. Pass them through a sieve before adding them to your bake, to make sure you've removed any lumps or bits of shell.

 ## Can I use any eggs for baking?

All bird eggs can be used in baking as they have similar properties, although they vary in size. If you are using large or small eggs in place of medium, for example, first beat them well, to combine the white and yolk, then use a weight of 50g mixed egg for each whole medium egg specified in the recipe. If your recipe uses only egg whites, or yolks, separate the eggs and use 35g of the white or 25g yolk per each medium egg in the recipe; add 5g more of each if a large egg is stipulated.

Any excess white or yolk can be used either as a glaze or, if there's a lot left over, it can be mixed with a tiny pinch of salt and frozen. In practice, though, it's easier to incorporate any leftover egg in a batch of scrambled eggs or an omelette.

If you are collecting eggs for baking from free-range birds, be sure to wash carefully any that come in from wet or muddy ground. Dry them thoroughly so that they don't go mouldy in the fridge. The egg shell is porous and may absorb unfriendly bacteria and flavours that could affect your baking. Bear in mind that if hens are fed strong-tasting vegetables, this flavour can transfer to the egg, especially garlic.

Can I bake without eggs?

It's hard to find substances to replace the role of eggs in cakes. This is because eggs help create the texture of the cake: the emulsifiers in the yolks and the proteins contained in the whites contribute to the strength of the cake crumb.

There are various natural, or naturally derived, substances that can be used in cake or tart recipes to mimic the texture of eggs – banana purée and tofu are two popular options. For baking purposes there are artificial egg substitutes based on potato starch and gums. These are particularly useful for people who have an allergy to eggs.

RECIPE SUBSTITUTIONS

 Can I use granulated instead of caster sugar?

Because granulated sugar and caster sugar are simply different-sized crystals of the same sugar, you would think you could use them more or less interchangeably. However, they don't acutally behave in the same way because granulated sugar doesn't dissolve as quickly as caster sugar when it's mixed with fat and liquid ingredients. This can cause problems when making sponge cakes – especially in creamed mixtures where the smaller grains of caster sugar allow more air to be incorporated into the mix. If you do use granulated sugar in creamed sponges, you'll notice an uneven surface texture and also that the sugar grains cause spotting because they have not dissolved very well.

Granulated sugar is less of a problem in whisked sponges as the sugar is more likely to dissolve in the liquid mixture (though it is still not as suitable as caster sugar). If you only have granulated sugar in the cupboard, the best thing to do is to make sure that it is fully dissolved before adding the flour to the mixture and baking. A trick you could try is to beat the sugar and eggs together lightly, and then leave them in a bowl over warm water for half an hour to soften the sugar before you whisk them fully.

Can I use icing sugar in place of caster sugar?

Icing sugar is not completely interchangeable with caster sugar, or granulated for that matter. This is because icing sugar is ground sugar mixed with anti-caking agents to stop it going lumpy. Interestingly, icing sugar available in the UK is more finely ground than that sold on the Continent, where icing sugar is more akin to finely ground caster sugar and still retains some texture.

Icing sugar can be used in place of caster sugar in any creamed, rubbed-in or melted mixtures as the anti-caking agent will be incorporated into the mixture. It's not advisable to use icing sugar in syrups.

 ## Can I bake cakes without sugar?

It may sound an odd question, but sugar is more important in some cakes than others. Sugar not only provides sweetness, it also affects the volume, colour and texture of a cake. While many cakes can't be made successfully without refined sugar, there are some alternatives for baking without it.

Some fruit cake recipes use puréed fruit, such as apricots, bananas and dates, to sweeten the mixture (see the recipe opposite). These fruits do still contain large amounts of sugar of course, just in a more natural form. You can also use honey or agave syrup in place of refined sugar as more natural sweeteners, although they are really just other forms of sugar. Honey contains the simple sugars glucose and fructose that the bee produces from the sucrose contained in nectar (see page 183 on how best to use honey in your recipes).

For a truly sugar-free bake, use sugar substitutes that are based on synthetic compounds. Most sugar substitutes are sweeter, weight for weight, than sugar, which means that if you choose to replace it, you will be using less of the substitute and may need to adjust your recipe to compensate for the lost volume and the difference in texture. Similarly, some substitutes, such as aspartame, may be affected by heat so may not work as well. Usually, the labelling of sugar substitutes will inform you how suitable they are for your own baking and you may just need to practise a few times to see what works.

•••

SUGAR-FREE FRUIT CAKE

Makes 1 cake
110g stoned prunes
50g dried apricots
225g plain flour
2 teaspoons baking powder
1 teaspoon ground cinnamon ½ teaspoon grated nutmeg
3 medium eggs

80ml sunflower oil
finely grated zest and juice of 1 orange
700g mixed chopped dried fruit
75g flaked almonds

1 x 20cm round, deep cake tin greased with butter
and lined with baking paper

✻ Preheat the oven to 180°C/350°F/gas 4. Cut up the prunes and apricots and simmer them in 120ml water until soft. Purée the fruit in a blender or food processor and cool.

✻ Sift the flour, baking powder and spices into a bowl. In another bowl, beat the eggs and oil together with the orange zest and juice. Finally, add the cooled fruit purée, flour mixture, dried fruit and almonds and mix well to combine evenly.

✻ Turn into the cake tin. Make a slight depression in the centre to prevent the cake doming. Bake for 45–55 minutes until a skewer inserted in the centre comes out clean. Cool in the tin for an hour before removing carefully. When fully cool, remove the paper and store in an airtight tin for a couple of days before cutting.

• •

Can I make a cake without fat?

To make a cake with no fat at all is pretty tricky, but cakes containing almost no fat can be made using only the egg white. These kinds of cakes are very pale and light; the angel food cake popular in America is one example. Here, egg whites are whisked to provide lift and to bind the cake, but because there is no egg yolk present to emulsify the mixture and lend moisture, the cake will stale quickly. Perfect for trifle, then!

A whisked sponge cake is another type of cake that contains a limited amount of fat. It does contain whole eggs, and therefore some fat, which exists in the egg yolk. However, it still contains much less than a creamed sponge, which usually consists of around 25 per cent fat.

ANGEL FOOD CAKE

This is traditionally baked in a tall domed mould, but can also be made in a ring-shaped cake tin.

Makes 1 ring-shaped cake
100g plain flour
300g caster sugar
300ml egg whites (from about 12 medium eggs)
1 teaspoon lemon juice or cream of tartar
1 teaspoon pure vanilla extract

1 x 25cm ring-shaped cake tin, greased with butter and lightly dusted with plain flour

❄ Preheat the oven to 180°C/350°F/gas 4. Sift the flour with half the sugar into a small bowl and set aside.

❄ Combine the egg whites and lemon juice or cream of tartar in the bowl of a free-standing electric mixer, or a large bowl if you are using a hand-held mixer. Beat until the whites form soft peaks. Add the remaining sugar all at once along with the vanilla extract, then continue beating until the mixture is glossy and you have stiff peaks.

❄ Using a large whisk or metal spoon, fold in the flour mixture a little at a time until it is all incorporated and there are no lumps.

❄ Transfer the mixture to the tin and place in the centre of the oven. Bake for 35–40 minutes until the cake is a medium brown and firm to a (light) touch. Transfer the cake, in its tin, to a wire rack and cool for 10 minutes. Then turn out and leave to cool completely. When cold, the cake can be decorated to your liking.

Variation: To make an enriched whisked sponge, or Genoese, melt 50g unsalted butter and add this to the mixture after the flour has been fully incorporated, folding it in gently.

•••

Can I use strong flour for cake-making?

Because strong or bread flour contains more gluten than plain and self-raising flours it is generally less suitable for cake-making. This is because the gluten will contribute additional elasticity to the mixture, making your cake tough and chewy – not an appealing prospect!

If you have to resort to using strong flour to make a sponge cake, the best thing to do is to handle the batter as gently as possible. Start by rubbing in the flour with the fat, as you would if you were making a scone mixture. This way, the gluten is less likely to be developed (made elastic) because the flour is combined with the fat before it comes into contact with moisture, which it needs to become elastic. You may also need to add extra liquid as strong flour absorbs more than plain flour.

TROUBLESHOOTING

 ## What happens if my oven isn't quite at the right temperature?

In order to cook through, all cakes need to reach an internal temperature of at least 90°C/195°F, and those that contain a high proportion of sugar will be cooked only when the temperature reaches 100°C/212°F. At this temperature, all of the starch in the cake will be fully cooked and the structure of the sponge strong enough to hold without collapsing.

The only way to ensure that cakes bake properly is to have the oven set to the correct temperature – writers and chefs do spend a lot of time testing recipes to make sure that they work after all!

Most sponges and cakes that are designed to have a light, airy texture should be cooked quickly – at a temperature of around 170–200°C/325–400°F. The higher temperature means that the starch can expand quickly at the same time as the fat melts, allowing the sponge to form properly and continue to expand evenly until the mixture sets. If you bake a large sponge cake at too low a temperature, you will end up with a dense cake that does not rise evenly and that might taste raw and look pallid.

How can I tell if my cake is ready?

All bakers have their own methods to check for doneness, using sight, smell and sometimes just plain instinct to tell whether a cake is ready or not. Of course, some methods are more scientific than others!

In fact the most reliable way of telling if your cake is ready is to measure its internal temperature using a temperature probe. This method is a great help for a beginner because there is nothing more crushing than making a cake that sinks as it cools. As mentioned in the previous question, the centre of a cake will reach 90–100°C/195–212°F when it is fully cooked.

Although recipes normally suggest a baking time, it is difficult to give precise guidelines. Ovens differ in their power and the speed at which they will cook a particular cake. Also, where you place a cake in the oven will affect the cooking – we have all come a cropper using an oven that has a hot spot to one side. This is just as true with fan ovens as it is with conventional or gas. And you should expect a cake to take longer to cook if you are baking more than one at a time.

When you are trying out a recipe for the first time, follow it to the letter, making sure you preheat the oven and arrange the shelves so that the cake can be placed in the centre. An oven thermometer is a very handy purchase as your oven's thermostat may be out by 10 degrees or so. Observe the cake as it bakes and, if the oven temperature in the recipe is correct, the cake should begin to brown only towards the end of the cooking time.

A cake that is baked at the correct temperature in the correct tin will rise evenly and the surface will darken and shrink slightly as it nears the end of the suggested time. The cooked cake will be set and gently resistant when pressed lightly. The smell of cooked cake is distinctive and, with experience, it will set off your own internal cake timer.

Another way to test if your cake is cooked is by using a thin skewer or wooden cocktail stick. When the cake has baked for the time designated in the recipe, remove it from the oven, insert the skewer into its centre, then gently pull it out again. If the cake is cooked, the skewer will come out clean. If raw cake mixture is attached to the skewer, you need to bake the cake a little more before retesting.

Small sponge cakes cooked in shallow sandwich tins will cook quickly – half an hour is usually plenty of time to cook this type of cake – while a deep cake, such as a Madeira cake, or a heavy, dense cake, such as a fruit cake, may take an hour or several respectively. The oven temperature for these types will be lower to allow the heat to penetrate through to the centre of the cake without overcooking the outer layers. The centre, though, will still need to come up to the required temperature before it is cooked.

 ## What if my cake is browning too much as it cooks?

If your cake is turning brown long before you expect it to be ready, the safest option is to reduce the oven temperature to 140°C/275°F/gas 1 (the original heat will hopefully have already activated the raising agents).

It is best to leave the cake at this temperature to finish baking – it might well take a little longer but better than having a burnt cake! To be sure it is done, test your cake with a temperature probe as recommended on page 43.

If you're still worried about it and your cake has quite a while still to bake, you can also lay a sheet of foil loosely over the surface of the cake, which will reflect heat and prevent it from burning.

How can I stop my creamed mixtures curdling?

There are two common reasons for a creamed mixture curdling or splitting. Firstly, your ingredients might be too cold. All of them should be at a warm room temperature before you begin, so take them out of the fridge well in advance. The butter needs to be very soft to be creamed successfully. If other ingredients, especially eggs, are cold, they will cool and harden the butter when mixed in. This makes it more likely that the emulsion between your butter and the liquid in the eggs will break down and split. You would then need to rewarm the mixture to regain the emulsion – which is possible but not without a good deal of bother.

Secondly, it may be that you have added the eggs too quickly. If you have ever made mayonnaise, you will know how important it is to add the egg slowly and beat the mixture thoroughly after each addition. Bear this principle in mind when you are making a cake too, as the mixture will trap good quantities of air only if the emulsion is maintained. Too much egg added at any one time will result in the emulsion breaking down, and the mixture will curdle, so add just a little at a time.

 ## Can I do anything to recover a curdled mixture?

You certainly can so there's no need to throw the mixture out with the eggshells! You can try adding another egg yolk to the mixture, or even a spoonful of warm water, both of which can help.

If you notice that the mixture looks as if it is about to curdle (it will look grainy), you can stir in a tablespoon of flour. If your mix does curdle, this doesn't mean the end of it: the baked cake will simply not be as light as it otherwise would have been, but it will taste just the same so don't start reaching for your bin.

 ## Why do cakes sometimes sink in the middle?

Watching a cake sink as it cools is possibly a baker's worst nightmare. If it happens, the centre can be hollowed out and used to hold a filling (or hidden under a thick layer of cream or icing!), or the cake can be cut into chunks and used in trifle. But why *has* it sunk?

Essentially, it is because the cake is underbaked. If the mixture has not heated through so that the egg, flour and fat structure is firm and fully cooked, the mixture will collapse back on itself and sink as it cools. Cakes sink in the centre because this is the last part of the cake to reach the temperature required to fully solidify the structure.

 ## Why has my cake domed?

The ideal shape for a sponge cake is flat, or perhaps very slightly domed. There are several reasons why a sponge cake may rise majestically in the centre as it bakes. Think back to the appearance of your cake mixture. Was it possible you made a mistake when weighing? If your cake mixture is too dry, it will set before the cake has fully expanded. The expansion will take place in the centre of the cake as this is the last part of the cake to cook fully. So when measuring your ingredients, be sure to weigh them carefully. A dry, stiff mixture may also be caused by using eggs that are too small. Check your recipe – if a number of eggs is given, ensure that this equates to the right weight of liquid. For example, if you are making a pound cake, or a cake where the eggs should make up 25 per cent of the weight of the cake mixture, be sure that the eggs do weigh that when cracked. To make up any difference you can add additional beaten egg or milk to the mix, but don't add more than 1 tablespoon of milk per egg used as any more will overly dilute the mixture.

CAKES AND BISCUITS

Another simple explanation is that you've used a cake tin that is too small. By doing so, the outer edge of the cake sets and stiffens as it reaches the top of the tin while the remaining cake mixture continues to cook and rise. The tin prevents it from pushing through the crust other than where it is softest – in the middle. This is why long-baked or deep sponge cakes sometimes erupt volcanically as the uncooked centre emerges through the lightly set crust of the middle.

 ## Why do my cakes stick?

The answer to this question may seem very simple but you'd be suprised how often a cake will stick to the inside of the tin if the tin isn't lined correctly. If you're an experienced baker you may feel you know how to do this properly, but it's always worth reminding yourself! First, grease the base of the tin, then the sides. Then cut a piece of baking paper to fit the base. If you also dust the inside of the cake tin with a small amount of plain or self-raising flour, you'll get a cleaner edge to your cake: it helps the cake mixture to rise evenly by creating a barrier between the batter and the tin and ensuring there are no air bubbles or gaps to interfere with the rise. (Dusting the flour inside also shows up any gaps in the greasing.)

For delicate sponges, cakes that contain a lot of sugar, or those cakes that require a longer bake, such as fruit cakes and deep sponges, it's always wise to line the sides of the cake tin too.

First, grease the tin well. Cut two pieces of paper to fit the base of the tin. Lay one in the base of the tin and lightly grease this. Then cut a strip for the sides 2cm wider than the height of the tin, and snip it at intervals along one edge. Fit the strip of paper around the sides, allowing the snipped edge to fold over onto the base. Grease the side strip. Finally, place the other cut sheet of paper on the base, on top of the snipped edge, and grease this.

For an extra layer of protection, the tin for fruit cakes, which are often in the oven for a couple of hours, can be wrapped on the outside with a sheet of brown paper, newspaper or foil, which slows the penetration of heat into the cake and prevents the outer layers from overcooking, or burning.

 ## Why have my glacé cherries sunk in my cake?

Fruit and other additions to a cake mixture may sink if the batter is too soft to support them, so the mixture is usually made denser or heavier to cope with this. (The typical cherry cake is made with a Madeira cake mixture, which has more flour than the usual creamed sponge.)

However, the type of batter is not always the problem; often it's the type and size or stickiness of the fruit used that's the reason for it sinking. Glacé cherries are notorious for this as they are generally large and sticky, so the best tip for cherries is to rinse and dry them thoroughly before tossing them in a little flour taken from the recipe.

A small scattering of other dried fruit, such as raisins, will be less likely to sink. They are less sticky and smaller so don't slip about in the mixture as easily. In the case of fresh fruit, such as apple, plum or rhubarb, a firmer mixture is best, such as a rubbed-in cake mixture which will absorb the moisture that escapes from the fruit as it bakes.

BISCUITS

....

 From biscotti to bourbons: where do biscuits fall in baking history?

The word 'biscuit' is derived from the Latin for 'twice-cooked' (*bis* meaning twice and *coctus* the past tense of the verb *coquere*, meaning to cook) Biscuits were originally hard, dry rusks made from plain doughs. Italian biscotti are a good, surviving example of the way that biscuits were traditionally made using early ovens: first by cooking a dough rather like a choux paste on the stove, or baking a firmer dough as a loaf, then cutting it and baking again to a crisp brittle biscuit.

It is possible that this technique grew out of a need to preserve cakes that would otherwise go off too quickly. In the medieval English court, a simple flour dough flavoured with rosewater or spices was made into thin wafers or biscuits. During his reign in the early sixteenth century, Henry VIII had a Wafery built at Hampton Court especially for the production of these thin and delicate sweet treats, the preserve of the Royal table.

Biscuits have often been used as a more durable source of ready-to-eat carbohydrate than bread. The unsweetened ship's biscuit used for centuries by sailors was baked not twice, but four times to ensure that it kept hard during long voyages. Even today, plain biscuits containing a good proportion of fat (for extra calories) are used in military and polar rations, although biscuits for popular consumption – whether sweet or savoury – are generally only baked once.

What's the difference between biscuits and cookies?

Although in Britain we tend to use these terms to denote more or less the same thing, we do make the distinction that cookies are larger than biscuits and underbaked so that they are still slightly soft in the centre rather than fully crisp. To Americans, a cookie is sweet and may be either soft or crisp, while what we call a savoury biscuit is called a cracker in the USA. And to further confuse things, their 'biscuit' is similar to our scone!

It is thought that cookies developed as test pieces of dough used for checking that the oven temperature was neither too hot nor too cool for baking a larger cake or bread (which would have been difficult to judge without modern thermometers).

One of the most popular cookies, the chocolate chip, was first invented in 1937 by Ruth Graves Wakefield, who ran a restaurant in Massachusetts called the Toll House. Such was the success of her cookies that Ruth's reputation spread and Nestlé began to manufacture bars of chocolate sold with a special cutter designed to cut chunks of chocolate that were the perfect size for the chips in the Toll House cookies. The recipe was printed on the inside of the wrapper.

 ## What are melted biscuits?

The melting technique resembles methods found in early biscuit recipes where ingredients were warmed together before being spooned onto trays for baking. Today we tend to use this method when we make biscuits that contain honey, syrup or treacle, which are difficult to blend with other ingredients when cold.

A melted biscuit dough can be firm – as in the case of gingernuts – or soft, such as for brandysnaps depending on the proportion of flour used. More flour gives a firmer, sturdier biscuit.

••

GINGERNUTS

Makes 45–50 biscuits
200g self-raising flour
2 teaspoons ground ginger
1 teaspoon ground cinnamon
100g Muscovado or golden caster sugar

75g salted butter
100g golden syrup
1 medium egg
2 tablespoons demerara sugar, for dredging

3–4 baking sheets, lined with baking paper

❋ Preheat the oven to 180°C/350°F/gas 4. Sift together the flour and spices and set to one side. Place the sugar, butter and syrup in a medium saucepan and set over a medium heat. Allow to melt gently – don't let the mixture boil. When melted, remove from the heat and leave to cool until just hand warm.

❋ Beat the egg thoroughly, then add to the sugar mixture. Finally, add in the flour mixture and beat well.

❋ Using a large teaspoon, place blobs of the mixture on the baking paper, spacing them at least 5cm apart. Sprinkle a little demerara sugar on top of each blob. Bake for 12–15 minutes until they feel firm and are dry to the touch. Transfer to a wire rack to cool.

• •

CAKES AND BISCUITS

Why do biscuits go soft?

All biscuits will soften if they are not stored in an airtight container, even savoury ones, simply because they will absorb moisture from the air. Biscuits that contain sugar of one kind or another soften more quickly because sugar is hygroscopic (this means that sugar absorbs water from the air).

Although we use a biscuit tin these days to keep our biscuits crisp, historically other devices have been invented not only to dry the biscuits once made, but also to store them. The 'breadflake' was one such example: this was a large vertical rack that would have been stood in front of an open fire. Biscuits or oatcakes could be stacked on it for drying rather like a giant magazine rack. When stored on a breadflake they would keep crisp for a long time.

So, what can you do if your biscuits have gone soft? The easiest way to refresh and crisp them again is to place them on a baking sheet and to warm them for 10 minutes in an oven preheated to 140°C/280°F/gas 2. Transfer them to a wire rack to cool and then put them into an airtight tin as soon as you can.

 ## Why is shortbread called a 'bread' when it's actually a biscuit?

The story of shortbread, too, begins in the twelfth century with the concept of baking bread twice to make a hard 'biscuit bread'. Over time, as biscuits evolved, the yeast in the dough was replaced by butter, which gave the bread a 'shorter' texture (see next question). This particular type of biscuit became known as shortbread.

 ## What does the 'short' in shortbread mean?

In the sixteenth century, flat, thin biscuits baked from a rich pastry containing eggs, with yeast for leavening, were known as 'short cakes' – 'short' being an old English word meaning 'crumbly' in texture. The term was also used to describe biscuits, and short or shortcrust pastry, with its high proportion of fat, is similarly named.

 ## Why does shortbread have tails?

The invention of shortbread is often attributed to Mary Queen of Scots, but it is unlikely that she ever got her hands in the mixing bowl. It is said that Mary was particularly fond of 'petticoat tails' – triangular segments cut from a large round shortbread that was originally flavoured with caraway seeds.

There are two surviving theories as to the origins of the description 'petticoat tail'. One is that the triangles were thought to resemble the triangular pieces of cloth used to make petticoats, known as 'petticoat tallies' – a 'tally' was the word for a pattern. However, the idea persists that the name is a corruption of the French *petites gatelles* ('little cakes').

Traditionally shortbread is made into one of three forms: tails, rounds and fingers, although it is now frequently shaped into more imaginative forms, usually in decorative moulds made from wood and intricately carved. Once turned out, the shortbread retains the imprint of whatever has been carved in relief on the inside of the mould. As shortbread dough is crumbly, it is easily pressed into a shape, and the pressure then consolidates the dough.

Shortbread dough can also be rolled out and cut into shapes (as in the recipe overleaf) using cutters.

••

SHORTBREAD

Old recipes for shortbread frequently include caraway seeds or other spices and usually some form of citrus peel. They are lovely and well worth trying. This recipe uses both.

You can either rub in the mixture using your fingers or blend together in a food processor. As there is virtually no water in the dough, there is no chance of developing the gluten in the flour, so the biscuits will be deliciously crisp and delicate whichever method you use.

Makes approximately 20 biscuits or two large shortbreads made with a 15cm-diameter mould

300g plain flour
200g unsalted butter, at room temperature
100g caster sugar
½ teaspoon caraway seeds
grated zest of 1 orange or ¼ teaspoon orange oil

2 baking sheets greased lightly with butter, shortbread mould (optional)

❋ Preheat the oven to 150°C/300°F/gas 2.

❋ Combine all the ingredients in a bowl and rub them together using your fingertips until you have an even, smooth dough. Alternatively, blend them together in a food processor.

❋ Roll out the dough on a lightly floured worktop to a thickness of 3–4mm.

❋ Cut into your desired shape, flouring your cutter well, or press into a floured mould.

❋ Transfer the cut biscuits to a baking sheet, spacing them 2–3cm apart. Bake for 25–30 minutes until they are evenly coloured light brown. If you are using a mould, invert it onto your baking sheet and remove, then bake the dough for 20 minutes before turning the oven down to 140°C/275°F/gas 1 and baking for a further 15–20 minutes.

❄ When you take the biscuits out of the oven, press them lightly with a fish slice or palette knife to consolidate them – this means that they will be crisp and less liable to be crumbly. Allow them to cool on the baking sheet for 5 minutes before you transfer them to a wire rack to cool fully.

• •

CHAPTER
TWO

BREAD

The huge variety of breads that we eat today, regardless of where we live, owe a lot to ancient methods and early ingredients. Sourdough and slow-fermented breads made with yeast, and griddle- and stone-baked soda breads, are some of the earliest types of leavened breads, invented by those without ovens, yet they now grace artisan bakeries across the country.

Although wheat flour is most widely used in British bread-making today, a whole host of regional variations were once enjoyed throughout the country; differences in landscape, weather, altitude and soil in our small islands meant that bread was made from what grew best locally. Barley, rye and oat flours were all widely used as the main grain in regions where wheat production wasn't possible or where these other grains were simply more productive. The oats is still dominant in Scottish agriculture and cuisine as it is one of the few grains to withstand their harsh winters, hence the continued popularity of oatcakes, one of the earliest forms of bread.

You need just four very simple ingredients to make bread: flour, yeast, salt and water. Above all, you also need time. Bread-making isn't something you should hurry. As this chapter explains, those ingredients all have defined roles in helping you to bake a perfectly risen loaf and they need to be given the time to work. Similarly, the stage of allowing your kneaded dough to rest and rise – prove – is vital in helping to ensure you bake a loaf with an evenly browned crust and a lovely chewy crumb with good flavour.

THE HUMBLE LOAF

 How did bread arrive in Britain?

The Romans introduced bread to the British Isles when they invaded in around 50 BC. They used a variety of grains, grinding them by hand to create different types of bread made from wheat, rye, acorns and groats. But it was not until the Middle Ages that bread-making really began to establish itself, and we can trace the development of a trade as bakeries began to open across Britain. It is perhaps strange to think that bread, something we take for granted as an everyday foodstuff, was at this time a status symbol. The bread consumed varied according to the grain affordable to each social class: the nobility ate soft, small loaves called manchets, made of the highest quality finely milled wheat; merchants enjoyed more rustic wheaten cobs, while the poor made do with bran loaves.

Hardship often forced medieval bakers to use their ingenuity to scrape together the necessary ingredients for their breads, leading to some less-than-pleasant results. When grains were scarce, powdered fish and animal bones were sometimes added to loaves to provide bulk. Unscrupulous bakers often used similarly unsavoury ingredients, including sawdust and sand, to bulk out their bread and increase their profits. But such practices were outlawed in London from around 1266, and regulated by the Bakers' Guild (formed around 1155 under Henry II). Such was the importance of bread in daily life that the Guild was given legal power to punish breadmakers for a variety of offences until as late as 1815, at which point regulatory power was taken over by Parliament.

The invention of the modern roller mill in the 1870s meant that wheat flour became commonly available and the white loaf became a staple in British diets.

 ## What are flatbreads?

The word 'flat' might make you think that these breads are not leavened, but in fact many of them do contain some sort of raising agent.

'Flatbread' is a general term used to describe thin, flat breads, often with a somewhat chewy texture, such as pitta, naan, chapaati and pizza. Flatbreads may also be crisp – Middle Eastern lavosh and Norwegian flatbrød are both crunchy.

The characteristic that unites flatbreads is their short cooking time: they are all cooked in direct contact with a very hot surface – a griddle or other pan, or the floor or wall of an oven. During the brief cooking, flatbreads may puff up – some slightly, others dramatically – but they don't rise as a yeasted bread dough does.

THE POWER OF FLOUR

 Does it matter whether I use strong flour or plain flour to make bread?

Every bread baker wants to open their oven and lift out a beautifully risen loaf with a good crumb, and their choice of flour is one of the most important elements in achieving this. It is the protein content in the flour, in the form of gluten (see opposite), that gives bread the strength to rise and affects the structure of the loaf's crumb.

Flour companies help bread makers by producing flours rich in the necessary proteins, which are labelled as 'strong' or 'bread' flour. You can see from the table below how much the protein content in the main types of flour varies, and why it so important to use the right flour:

Flour type	Protein content
Plain (and self-raising)	8–10 per cent
Strong or bread	12–16 per cent
Durum wheat	12–16 per cent

Extra-strong bread flour (white and wholemeal) is also widely available, and usually made from Canadian flour with 15–16 per cent protein. It's most often used for making bagels and for bread with a bread-maker where kneading is reduced and the dough is usually proved only once. The dough can absorb more water and rise higher to make a bigger, lighter-textured loaf.

Most wheat bread recipes need flours with about 12 per cent protein content. Bread made using flour other than strong bread flour won't rise as much and could be heavier, flatter and denser, as it is in Irish soda bread, for example, which uses flour with less protein. The best baguettes are made from French flour with a slightly lower protein content than British bread flour, as this allows the crust to crack when the dough can't rise any more and it tears when it's over-stretched. Flour with lower protein content can also be used for sweet bread doughs as these contain other ingredients which lighten the dough and help them to rise (see page 96).

 ## What is gluten and why is it important?

Flour contains two proteins: gliadin and glutenin. When liquid is added to these proteins and mixed, the gliadin and glutenin molecules bond with each other and in the presence of oxygen form gluten, which in turn determines the structure of the bread. While the gliadin bonds are weak, glutenin has the ability to organise itself into a strong network of chains that are not easily broken – this is known as the gluten network.

The gluten network can be stretched and becomes more elastic as it is kneaded. It is this elasticity that gives the dough the strength to retain the carbon dioxide produced by the yeast, thus allowing the dough to rise and hold its shape as it proves then bakes (see page 69).

Can I substitute other types of flour for wheat?

Almost all grains contain gluten, including spelt, barley and rye, but in different quantities and types. Spelt flour performs much like wheat flour so is reasonably interchangeable in spite of the fact that the gluten content is lower. It is possible to make bread from either barley or rye flour on their own, but both will have very different qualities to a wheat loaf. Barley flour will produce a slightly grey, flat bread while rye will be sticky and very difficult to handle. If you are interested in trying these flours, start off by using them to replace 25 per cent of the white wheat flour in a standard recipe and go from there – just enjoy experimenting!

Why is it more difficult to make wholemeal bread?

Wholemeal flour contains all the parts of the whole-wheat grain, or berry. The wheatgerm and bran left in the flour add flavour and texture, as well as nutrients, but the bran component of wholemeal flour can also make wholemeal doughs hard to knead as the small, relatively brittle pieces of bran disrupt the formation of a strong gluten network. Additionally, bran absorbs water slowly, so that the dough tends to dry as you work it.

The key to making a good wholemeal loaf is to add the correct amount of liquid (which can be 10–20 per cent more than is required for a white dough), and to use a different kneading technique. Rather than kneading continuously, it is better to knead wholemeal dough in three or four short bursts. This allows the gluten network to build gradually while being less disrupted by the bran, resulting in a lighter, well-risen loaf.

How is gluten-free flour made and can it be used to make good bread?

Grains such as rice contain proteins that can do a similar job to gluten, and so gluten-free flour is usually made up of rice flour plus small quantities of potato, tapioca and buckwheat flours. Plant gums are used to create the bonds that mimic the structure of the gluten network (see above).

Gluten-free flour will make a reasonable loaf, but the flour tends to require more water and the other ingredients need to compensate for the lack of gluten in order for the loaf to rise. It's best to follow a recipe that has been created using gluten-free flour.

Does flour go off?

Look at a bag of flour and you will see it has a 'best before 'or 'use by' date. While it is true that flour will keep almost indefinitely as long as it is stored in a cool dry place, the flavour of the flour will deteriorate, especially wholemeal flour. This is because wholemeal flour contains a small amount of fat that isn't present in white flour, and which can turn rancid over time. Buy flour as you need it. The ideal keeping time for a bag of flour is a month. Obviously this isn't always practical, but the fresher the flour, the better the flavour your bread will have.

THE PROPERTIES OF YEAST

 **What is yeast?**

A yeast is a living organism; it is in fact a type of fungi. Yeast cells cover the surface of many foods, including grains and fruits and given the chance – with some moisture, a little warmth and food (in the form of flour or sugar) – yeast will start to grow.

 How does yeast help to make a dough rise?

Yeast converts the starch in flour into simple sugars – maltose and then glucose – which it uses as fuel or food. As it feeds, the yeast produces waste products, including alcohol and carbon dioxide. The creation and then expansion of this carbon dioxide gas is what makes the dough rise. The gas bubbles become trapped by the dough (in the gluten network, see page 65), which then sets around them as the loaf bakes.

Yeast is most active at warm temperatures (see pages 78–79) so this process will occur most rapidly if you make your bread in warm conditions. A cold room will slow the yeast activity, and in some cases, halt it altogether.

Is fresh yeast better than dried?

Neither is 'better' and you can use them in the same way; the two types simply have slightly different properties. Dried yeast (sold in two different forms, see next question) is still alive, just dormant and has been mixed with additives such as amylase, an enzyme, and ascorbic acid, which are included to make it work quickly. Fresh yeast may simply take a little longer to get going and two rises will produce a better loaf than a single rise.

If you are following a recipe that uses fresh yeast and want to substitute dried yeast, the simple formula is to use half the weight. In other words, if the recipe calls for 14g fresh yeast, replace this with 7g dried yeast. By volume, 7g is 1 ½ teaspoons, measured level. A sachet of fast-action yeast normally weighs 7g.

 ## What is the difference between regular and fast-action dried yeast?

Regular dried yeast needs to be soaked in water before use, whereas fast-action dried yeast (also called easy-blend or instant) can be sprinkled directly onto the flour and other dry ingredients. When liquid is then added (usually warm), the fast-action yeast produces carbon dioxide bubbles quickly and energetically.

Fast-action yeast is usually blended with flour improver, enzymes and additives that make the yeast work more quickly than regular dried yeast or fresh yeast, thus a loaf will need only one rising, rather than the usual two.

Although this type of yeast can be convenient, because of the added flour improvers and enzymes, and the speed at which it works, it can work less well in traditional recipes and affect the texture of the finished loaf. Loaves made with fast-action dried yeast can have a drier texture than loaves made with fresh or regular dried yeast, especially if too much is used.

 ## Why is yeast sometimes referred to as brewer's yeast?

If you get a chance to look around an old manor house, you'll see that the brew house and bakery are often next door to each other. This is because bakers and brewers used to work hand in hand.

When traditional ale is produced, a yeasty froth gathers on top of the fermenting liquid, known as 'the wort'. This used to be scooped off, washed and added to the bread dough to leaven it. The leavening yeast was known as 'barm' and bread made this way was sweeter than bread made using modern-day yeast. Recipes printed as late as the 1880s advised the home cook to make sure that the 'barm' for their bread-making was sweet and clean, from a fresh brew, rather than old and strongly flavoured, which would not make good bread.

In the nineteenth century, this process was refined and industrialized to enable us to manufacture the yeast we use today for baking bread.

• •

A SIMPLE WHITE LOAF

Makes 2 large loaves
800g strong white bread flour
14g fresh yeast or 7g sachet dried yeast or
    7g sachet fast-action dried yeast
2 teaspoons salt
550ml water at 30°C/85°F

2 x 1kg bread tins, greased with butter or lard

❋ Place the flour in a large bowl and, if using fast-action dried yeast, stir in the salt thoroughly before adding the fast-action dried yeast.

❋ If using fresh yeast or dried yeast, in a small bowl, wet the yeast with a little of the warm water and stir it to a cream. Add the remaining water, then add this mixture to the flour. Mix well together.

❋ Tip the mixture onto a clean worktop. Knead for 10–15 minutes until the dough is shiny and elastic. Don't worry if it sticks to your hands initially; just keep cleaning them with a plastic scraper. Try not to add a significant quantity of extra flour to prevent the dough from sticking – this will only make the dough firm up and dry slightly.

✳ Put the dough back in the bowl and cover with a damp cloth. Leave the dough to rise at a warm, but not hot, room temperature for 1–2 hours until it has doubled in size.

✳ Turn out the dough onto a lightly floured worktop and knead it for 2–3 minutes to even it out. Divide the dough into two equal portions. Knead each lightly to form a cylinder that has a crease at its base. Place in the tins crease down and cover them with a damp tea towel. Leave the loaves to rise at the same warm room temperature for 45–60 minutes until they have doubled in size – this will be when the dough just mounds over the rim of the tins by 1–2cm.

✳ Preheat the oven to 220°C/425°F/gas 7 and adjust the shelves so that the loaves have room to rise.

✳ When the oven is hot, remove the tea towel and sprinkle the loaves with a little flour. Carefully slice a shallow groove along the centre of each loaf. Place in the oven and bake for 20 minutes, then turn the loaves around so that they cook evenly. Reduce the temperature to 180°C/350°F/gas 4 and bake for a further 20–25 minutes.

✳ The loaves are ready if they sound hollow when tapped on the base.

✳ Turn the loaves out onto a wire rack and allow them to cool fully before using. When cold, store in an airtight tin for up to three days. You can also try these variations:

For milk bread:
Replace the water with full-fat milk.

For a rich loaf:
Replace the water with 450ml full-fat milk and add 100g softened butter and 1 egg, beaten, which should be added to the flour with the yeast and milk mixture.

For baps:
Use half milk and half water and add 50g butter or lard cut into small chunks which should be added to the dough along with the liquids and kneaded together.

Divide the risen dough into 18 even balls and roll each into a flat disc. Leave to rise for another 30 minutes, then bake in a preheated 200°C/400°F/gas 6 oven for 20 minutes.

••

 ## Why shouldn't I mix yeast directly with salt or sugar?

Yeast is a very simple living organism and as such it is easily affected by what you do to it. Strong ingredients such as sugar and salt will kill the yeast if they come into direct contact with it. Recipes, therefore, usually tell you to mix the salt or sugar into the flour or a liquid before combining with the yeast, so that the yeast only comes into contact with a dilute concentration of either.

MAKING BREAD

 What does kneading do to bread?

When a bread dough is kneaded, either by hand or in a large free-standing electric mixer using the dough hook, it is repeatedly stretched, folded and compressed. This kneading action strengthens the gluten network, making the dough elastic. The more stretchy the dough, the more carbon dioxide gas it can hold within the gluten network, creating a greater rise.

If you don't knead the dough and bake it after a short rise, you will still have an edible bread, but the loaf may be flat and the texture will be dense. There are, in fact, bakers who advocate no-knead bread, claiming that it has a superior taste. One such influential baker and British nutritionalist Doris Grant, author of *Your Daily Bread* (1944), did much to popularise this method – although it came about entirely by accident. Grant argued that kneading diminished the flavour and texture of bread (a fact she had discovered after forgetting to knead her wholemeal dough before baking it). To prove her point she created a simple wholemeal loaf that isn't kneaded but is moist, nutty and keeps well.

THE GRANT LOAF

The structure of breads like the Grant loaf differs from that of a kneaded bread – they won't have the springy texture. Instead, they will be more like a loaf made using low-gluten flour, or soda bread.

Makes 3 large loaves
1.5kg stoneground wholemeal flour
14g fresh yeast or 1 x 7g sachet dried yeast
   or 1 x 7g sachet fast-action dried yeast
15g salt, or more to taste
 1.2 litres water, at 35–38°C/95–100°F
3 teaspoons brown sugar or honey

3 x 1kg loaf tins, greased and warmed

❋ Place the flour in a large bowl and, if using fast-action dried yeast, stir in the salt thoroughly before adding the fast-action dried yeast. (In very cold weather, warm the flour slightly – enough to take off the chill).

❋ If using fresh or dried yeast, place 3 tablespoons of the warm water in a cup and add the fresh or dried yeast. Leave for 2 minutes for the yeast to soak, then add the sugar or honey. In about 10–15 minutes this should have produced a thick, creamy froth. Put this into the flour and add the rest of the water.

❋ Mix well – by hand is best – for a minute or so, working from sides to middle, until the dough feels elastic and leaves the sides of the mixing bowl clean; this helps to make a well-built loaf.

❋ Divide the dough, which should be slippery, but not wet, into the loaf tins that have been warmed and greased. Put the tins in a warm place, cover with a cloth and leave for about 20 minutes until the dough is within 1cm of the top of the tins. (Even in a modern house, this might take longer than 20 minutes and up to 45 minutes depending on the how warm your house is.)

❋ Preheat the oven to 200°C/400°F/gas 6. Bake for 30 minutes then turn the oven down to 170°C/325°F/gas 3 and bake for a further 30 minutes. (A loaf of this size can take a while longer than the recipe suggests and every oven is different. Allow 1 hour, and then test the bread using a probe: the core of the loaves should register 90°C/195°F or more.)

••

 ## How will I know if I have kneaded my dough sufficiently?

Most bread recipes suggest a kneading time of 10 minutes by hand (6–7 minutes with a mixer) to achieve a satiny-smooth, elastic dough. Hand kneading may take more or less time than this, depending on how energetically you work the dough. So it is useful to have another guide by which to check if your dough is thoroughly kneaded. One test is to take a golf-ball size piece of dough and stretch it between your fingers until it forms a thin, translucent sheet. If it tears easily or is too firm to stretch, it isn't ready and you'll need to carry on kneading.

 ## Can I speed up the dough proving time?

Proving is the process of leaving the dough aside for a certain period – it activates the yeast and causes the dough to rise. To speed up the proving time, you need to activate the yeast faster. Yeast responds to food, moisture and warmth and will grow more rapidly if more food is available (see page 69, for more on yeast). It also works most quickly at a specific temperature – 35°C/95°F. However, the waste products (such as alcohol) that yeast expels at this temperature are strongly flavoured and if you leave your bread dough to rise at this high temperature, you run the risk of masking the delicate taste of the flour you have used to make the dough.

This is why most bakers prefer to prove their bread dough at cooler temperatures, between 20–24°C/ 68–75°F (warm room temperature), for longer, to get the perfect balance of texture and flavour.

There are ways to hurry things along a little bit, without affecting the flavour. If you mix some additional sugar with the liquid (approximately 1 teaspoon per 250ml) before adding the yeast to it, this extra 'food' will help the yeast get a little head start. Additives such as ascorbic acid (vitamin C) are also often used to give the yeast a boost, as are enzymes such as amylase (these are both added to fast-action yeasts, which is why they work more quickly than fresh or ordinary dried yeasts).

 ## How do I slow down the rising of my dough?

Alternatively, you might want to slow down the rate of development of your bread dough because you don't have the time to bake it from scratch all in one go.

One way of reducing the speed at which dough develops is to use less yeast – and to use fresh yeast not dried (see page 70). If you use half the amount of yeast specified in the recipe you will double the proving time. Bear in mind, though, that if you use too little yeast, the bread will take so long to develop that other microbes may grow and alter the flavour of your loaf.

Bakers often slow the fermentation deliberately, taking 1–2 days, to achieve a deeper, richer flavour. Anything longer, say a fermentation that lasts for 2–3 days, will lead to a very different bread, more reminiscent of a sourdough (see page 88).

 ## What does 'knocking back' mean?

Recipes often tell you to 'knock back' or 'punch down' your dough after it has had its first rise (prove). Although it sounds violent, this just means giving the dough a light knead before you shape it. This kneading remixes the components of the dough and reorganises the gluten network (see page 65), breaking down large, uneven gas bubbles, so that the shaped loaf will rise evenly a second time and then again during baking.

How can I tell if my bread dough is perfectly risen?

Many recipes tell you to leave your dough to rise for a specific number of hours. But rising can take different lengths of time, depending on the temperature of your ingredients when you began. Recipes also often tell you to leave the loaf to rise until it reaches the top of the tin. But not all tins are the same size – you might have two with the same capacity yet one is deeper or longer.

To ensure your dough has had enough time to rise, leave it until it has doubled in size. You do, of course, need to take note of what the dough looked like when you first left it to rise, so that you will know when it has doubled.

Watching and testing the spring of your dough as it rises is also useful. The consistency of the dough will change during this process. When a loaf is first shaped and put into its tin, the gluten will be full of elastic energy and will bounce back, feeling firm. As the dough rises some of this elastic energy will dissipate and the dough will feel less firm. It will also feel spongier because of the amount of carbon dioxide it now contains as a result of the fermentation.

There will come a point in its development when the dough no longer springs back when gently pressed with a fingertip. At this point it is ready to bake. If you leave the loaf to rise any longer, it will be over-proved. What may happen then is that the production of carbon dioxide exceeds the ability of the gluten network to hold the gas as distinct bubbles, which will then cause the loaf to collapse. If the loaf does not collapse, it will be very uneven once baked and, more likely than not, will be flat on top, rather than nicely rounded.

BAKING YOUR LOAF

 Why is bread always baked in a hot oven?

When you put your loaf into the oven, the heat needs to be high enough to start the bread rising and expanding immediately. This so-called 'oven spring' occurs in the first 5–10 minutes of baking. It stops when the bubbles trapped in the dough are fully expanded and the heat of the oven has killed the yeast cells and set the starch in the outer layers of the bread (this gets the drying and browning of the crust started). So it's important to make sure the oven is fully heated to the temperature specified in the recipe (some recipes even suggest heating it slightly higher than that specified and then reducing it after you place your loaf inside as some heat will be lost when you open the oven door).

 Why do some recipes suggest creating steam in the oven when baking bread?

A steamy atmosphere in your oven at the beginning of baking will influence the texture and appearance of your loaf. The steam condenses on the relatively cool loaf, forming a layer of water. This layer slows the crust formation, preventing it from becoming rigid, and the loaf can expand for longer before the crust starts to develop.

Professional bakers often inject steam into their ovens, but you can easily mimic this at home. Simply pre-warm a sturdy roasting tin in the bottom of the oven and then, when the loaf is placed in the hot oven, quickly pour a small glass of hot water into the roasting tin (be careful not to hit the hot shelf with your hand) and shut the oven door immediately. Pour in another glass of hot water before the first 5 minutes of baking are over.

 ## How can I tell if my loaf is baked?

Because oven temperatures can vary, and different baking tins give different results, it is helpful to know how to check if a loaf is cooked through. The traditional way is to tip the loaf out of the tin and tap the base. A clear, hollow sound indicates that the loaf is evenly cooked through, whereas a dull thud means the loaf needs more baking.

A more precise way to test if your loaf is cooked is to use a temperature probe. When the loaf has baked for the suggested cooking time, remove it from the oven, then insert the probe into the centre to check the internal temperature. To be thoroughly cooked, the loaf should register at least 90°C/195°F.

Why does my loaf have a hole running down the middle?

We've all seen this, even with commercial bread: when you slice a loaf, you discover a hole or tunnel running through the middle, as if a mouse has eaten its way through it. There are three possible reasons for this.

First, the dough may have been too floury when shaped. Usually, a tin loaf is shaped by rolling the dough into a neat cylinder, then it is placed in the tin with the crease underneath so that the shaped loaf rises evenly. If you've used too much flour at the shaping stage, the dough won't bond as it rises, leaving a hole when it is baked.

The second, more common, reason is that the loaf is under-baked. When a loaf is put into a hot oven the starch component of the flour is transformed by the oven heat from a soft gel to a firm sponge. The centre of a loaf needs to reach around 90°C/194°F for this to occur fully, so it ends up light and airy, not damp and dense. If it doesn't get hot enough during baking, when the loaf is cooled the heavy centre will shrink back to the firm, fully baked outer layers of the loaf, leaving a hole in the middle.

The last reason is that the loaf may not have been kneaded enough, which means the gluten structure won't have been properly developed, the distribution of carbon dioxide gas bubbles will not have been even and consequently the dough will not have risen evenly.

How can I make a crustier loaf?

The crust on a loaf of bread is often the best bit – so much so that the cuts on some bread shapes are made especially to develop as much crust as possible. If you want to make a loaf with a good crust, you have to choose the right type of bread and bake it in a certain way.

Professional bakers have several ways of achieving a good crust. First, they usually bake on a solid-floored oven. You can mimic this by using a baking stone: preheat it in the oven, then slip the bread onto the stone for baking. A strong baking sheet, preheated, will also do the job. Baking on a hot surface will ensure that the base of the loaf bakes thoroughly and ends up crusty.

Secondly, to ensure that the top of the loaf becomes well browned, professional bakers add steam to the oven during the first 5 minutes or so of baking (see also page 82).

A longer bake also ensures that a good thick crust forms. The outer surface of the loaf reaches and stays at a higher temperature for longer than the centre so a higher proportion of it is dried out, creating a thicker crust than there would have been for a shorter bake.

Bread doughs enriched with fat, eggs or milk won't make crusty loaves because the fat and lecithin contained within these ingredients will soften the crust. For a good crust, the best recipe to use is a straight flour, water, yeast and salt mixture.

What is the 'perfect crumb'?

'Crumb' is the term that bakers use to describe the inside of a loaf of bread. Bakers talk of trying to achieve the 'perfect crumb', which usually means a well-risen loaf with an even, light texture. If the dough is too dry, the texture of the bread will be close and tight. This is because the dough is too firm to allow the carbon dioxide bubbles to expand properly during the rising process, which results in a heavy crumb.

The temperature at which a dough is risen will also affect the evenness of the crumb. Ideally, a loaf should be allowed to rise at a moderate room temperature (see page 78) so heat will penetrate the dough gradually. If the temperature is too high, the outer layers of the loaf will develop too quickly, resulting in an uneven crumb with many different sizes of bubble – this is one reason why you should to knock back a risen dough (see page 79).

 ## What's the best way to store bread?

To keep homemade bread as fresh as possible you need to prevent moisture loss otherwise it will stale quickly. To do so, store it at room temperature in a bread box or other sealed container (not plastic) that will keep it airtight. Bought loaves should not be kept airtight because they have a high water content so are more susceptible to sweating and going mouldy if kept in an airtight container. Bread kept in the fridge will lose moisture more quickly than bread kept at room temperature as the cold draws it out, so don't store bread in the fridge unless you are intending to use it for toast. If you make a loaf and don't intend to eat it all within 2–3 days, cut it in half, wrap one half tightly and freeze it as soon as it is cool.

To freshen bread that has begun to age, spray the surface with a little water and reheat in a low oven. Don't heat it too much or you'll dry it out further. Allow the loaf to cool and firm before slicing.

SOURDOUGH

 What is sourdough?

Sourdough is the name used to describe a bread that is leavened using a sourdough starter or culture. The starter is made up of wild yeasts, which are gathered from natural sources (such as the air and in flour), rather than the purified, manufactured varieties. A portion of the starter is mixed with the bread ingredients and the resulting sourdough bread derives much of its flavour from the yeasts.

 Are sourdoughs really sour?

Sourdough is, in a way, a misnomer because not all naturally leavened breads are 'sour'. In technical terms, all will be mildly acidic – that is, of a low pH value – but that doesn't mean they will necessarily taste sour or acidic.

So where does the sourness come from and how can we control it? Wild yeasts contain a variety of yeast types whereas the fresh or dried yeast we normally use contain a single type. This variety contributes additional flavour to the bread as well as influencing its texture and acidity. A good deal of the difference in the flavour of sourdough loaves lies in how the sourdough starter or 'leaven' is treated and maintained and how the fungi and bacteria levels are balanced (see the next question).

 ## Can I make my own sourdough starter or leaven?

Absolutely! You can 'grow' your own wild yeast at home to make a sourdough starter. All you need is a suitable source of 'food', water, an ambient room temperature (18°C/64°F to 23°C/73°F) and a little time. In about 2 weeks you should be able to bake your loaf.

The 'food' can be a stoneground organic rye or a wheat and rye flour mix. This is minimally processed, meaning that more varieties of yeast will be present in the resulting starter.

To maintain a healthy starter you need to provide conditions that favour the yeasts (fungi), and that limit the growth of bacteria. The way to do this is to refresh the starter with fresh flour and water each day – known as 'feeding' it – and to keep your starter at room temperature. It is this balance that is the driver behind sourdough success. You need both the fungi and the bacteria, but in the right proportions. It can be tricky to get the balance right, which is why making sourdough does take practice.

Why is it important to keep the bacteria count in my starter low?

Bacteria adds flavour but it also secretes an enzyme into the starter as it grows which, if left unchecked, would destroy the gluten in the flour. No gluten would mean no gluten network and the resulting loaf would be heavy and flat (for more on gluten and the gluten network see page 65).

SOURDOUGH STARTER

Makes approximately 300g
100g organic rye flour, plus more for feeding
170ml water, boiled and cooled, plus more for feeding

❋ Combine the flour and water in a 1-litre bowl. Beat the ingredients together well until there are no lumps, then scrape the sides of the bowl clean, making a mound of batter in the base of the bowl.

❋ Take note of how the batter smells and looks, then cover the bowl loosely with a clean tea towel and leave it at an ambient room temperature. The wild yeast cells present in the flour will absorb water from the batter, rehydrate and come back to life from their dormant state.

❋ After 24 hours, beat the mixture well, then re-cover.

You may not notice much action in your batter for a day or two, but you will probably notice a change in the smell. Lift the tea towel and sniff carefully. If the yeast has begun to metabolise the starches, your nose should detect a sharp whiff of carbon dioxide and alcohol.

❉ For the next 4 days (6 days in total), beat the mixture once a day, then re-cover.

❉ If, after 3 or 4 days, the batter remains inert, or if white, black or green moulds grow on the surface, throw it away and start again with fresh flour and water. Getting the balance right does take practice and for whatever reason, your flour could be free from viable yeast cells – odd, but it can happen – or the conditions for activating the yeast weren't quite right (see page 89). But don't despair, if your original batter has failed to activate, try mixing the batter recipe again. Cover loosely with a tea towel and leave as before in a warmish place.

❉ Assuming that on day 6 you have now isolated a lively mixture of yeasts, you can build up the vigour of the cultures by continually refreshing the mixture with water and flour over the following week or so. Each day, pour away half the starter and add half the initial quantities of flour and water.

❉ By day 12, you should have a vigorous, fresh starter that is populated with a healthy variety of yeasts, with additional bacteria present in sufficient numbers to add flavour but not too much acidity.

••

BREAD

Where should I keep my starter?

The best place is in a loosely closed, rather than a tightly sealed, jar. (If your starter is very active it will grow quite substantially and may spill over the rim of the jar so do keep an eye on it.) If you're using your starter to make bread regularly you will be harvesting and feeding it every day. However, once the yeast and bacteria present have used up any available food, they will go dormant and wait for conditions to improve (i.e. for you to feed them and then harvest them again for baking). If you're not using your starter straightaway, you can maintain it in this dormant state in the fridge for a few days. To reactivate it, simply bring it back to room temperature and start the feeding process again. After a few days it should be bubbly and ready for use again.

Don't freeze your starter, though, because many of the yeast cells will be killed in the process.

 ## Why does my starter sometimes smell bad?

Sourdough that smells overly sour or bad – like stale beer or wine – has been over- or under-fed. Overfeeding it allows the starter to build up too large a population of bacteria and it becomes contaminated with too many yeast by-products. In an under-fed starter, the acid–yeast balance is wrong: the acid dominates and the starter will smell overly acidic (the yeast will also eventually die).

A properly refreshed starter will smell pleasantly acidic. If your starter does begin to smell bad, the best thing to do is to throw it away and start again with fresh flour and boiled water.

••

SOURDOUGH BREAD

Makes 1 large or 2 small loaves
500g organic strong white bread flour
15g fine salt
250g sourdough starter (see page 90)
250ml water, at room temperature
coarse semolina and additional flour, for dusting

❋ Mix the flour with the salt in a large bowl. Separately, mix the starter and water together until well blended. Add to the flour and stir to amalgamate. When nearly mixed, tip out onto a lightly floured board. Knead the dough with both hands until it is even and there are no lumps of flour. Don't worry if the dough is quite wet; it will firm up as the flour absorbs the water fully and the gluten develops.

❋ Knead the dough, occasionally scraping it from your hands, until it is shiny and very elastic. This can take up to 15 minutes, so you may want to consider using a large free-standing electric mixer fitted with a dough hook. Place the dough in a large bowl, cover with a damp, clean tea towel and leave to rise at room temperature for 2–3 hours until it has doubled in size.

✤ Turn out the dough onto a lightly floured surface and shape into one large or two small balls. Dust a clean, dry, coarse tea towel with a mixture of 1 tablespoon each of flour and semolina, rubbing the mixture into the surface of the cloth. Line one large or two small baskets or colanders with the cloth. Place the ball(s) of dough, crease uppermost, in the basket(s). Draw the cloth gently over the dough, then leave to rise again until doubled in size. This will probably take 2 hours.

✤ When the dough is nearly ready, preheat your oven to 220°C/425°F/gas 7. Arrange the shelves so that they will give the loaf or loaves space to rise and put a roasting tin in the base of the oven if you want a crusty loaf. Place a sturdy baking sheet for each loaf in the oven to preheat.

✤ When the loaf is risen and the oven is hot, open up the cloth and sprinkle the dough with a little flour (this will be the base of the loaf). Transfer the loaf to the baking sheet, ensuring the crease of the dough is on the bottom.

✤ Slash the top of the loaf carefully using a sharp, serrated knife or razor blade (this will allow the loaf to expand quickly), then put the loaf in the oven. If you want a crustier loaf, follow the advice about adding steam on page 82, but be careful not to use so much water that it causes the oven to cool down.

✳ Bake a large loaf for 50 minutes, turning the oven down to 180°C/350°F/gas 4 after 30 minutes. Bake small loaves for 30–35 minutes only. Test for readiness by tapping the bottom of the loaf. If it sounds hollow, and is well browned and firm, it is cooked through. Remove the loaf to a wire rack and allow it to cool fully before cutting.

• •

SWEET DOUGHS

 What sorts of sweet breads can I bake?

The great British 'bun' is perhaps the best example of a bread made from a sweet dough. Plump, spicy fruited sugary buns have been made in this country since at least the fifteenth century and many of our traditional buns, such as the sticky Chelsea, Bath and Marlborough buns, are named after the places in which they were first made and became fashionable.

Other popular buns were made for special celebrations, often associated with the Church. The most obvious example that comes to mind is the hot cross bun, which was made to be eaten on Good Friday. Hot cross buns should be rich in spice and heavy with fruit, butter and citrus – a luxury treat.

The word 'bun' has been used in English since the fifteenth century and is thought to derive from the old French word *bugne,* meaning 'swelling', which describes its shape. A bun used to refer to a quantity of bread rather than a specific type, which meant that buns could be either hard or soft, but from the early twentieth century the word 'bun' came to mean 'a bread made from a soft, sweetened yeasted dough'.

You might notice that some sweet dough recipes sometimes call for plain flour rather than the strong flour normally used for bread. The lower protein and gluten content give a more delicate, yielding crumb; the dough will rise just as well, but will be lighter and more cake-like than a traditional bread dough. To further soften the dough and to enrich it, milk powder, eggs and butter can be added, as in the Sally Lunn or Bath bun. The French brioche is another example of a heavily enriched sweet dough. Its high egg and butter content gives it a rich and soft crumb.

 ## What is a Sally Lunn?

The Sally Lunn is a light, rich round tea bun that has been made in Britain for at least 300 years. Its exact origins, and quite how it came to be named are unclear and historians have put forward several theories.

Some say there was indeed an original baker called Sally Lunn, who owned a pastry shop and shouted about her wares in the street. The bun was created to commemorate her. Others claim the recipe bears strong resemblance to a French Alsatian bake called *solilem.*

Most sources do agree, however, that the bun comes from France, that it should be made with cream or milk to enrich the dough and a little lemon zest or mixed spice, and ought to be eaten sliced and spread with clotted cream or butter. It can be made as one large bun or several small ones.

SALLY LUNN BUN

Makes one 22cm bun
15g fresh yeast or 1 x 7g sachet dried yeast
   or 1 x 7g sachet fast-action dried yeast
3 tablespoons milk at room temperature
350g strong flour
1 tablespoon caster sugar
1/2 teaspoon salt
180ml double cream,
   warmed to 30ºC in a small pan
3 medium eggs at room temperature
grated zest of 1/2 unwaxed lemon
   or 50g candied lemon peel

for the glaze
3 tablespoons milk
2 tablespoons caster sugar

1 x 22cm springform cake tin, greased
with butter and lined with baking paper

❉ If using fresh or dried yeast, place the yeast and milk
in a small bowl and add a large pinch of the flour. Leave
this in a warm place for 10 minutes, or until the yeast
begins to froth. Mix the remaining flour, sugar and salt
together in a large bowl. If using fast-action dried yeast,
add it to the bowl of flour after you have mixed in the
sugar and salt.

✳ Heat the cream in a small pan until it reaches 30°C/80°F, then add the eggs and beat in the lemon zest until the eggs are thoroughly blended.

✳ Mix the egg mixture, and yeast mixture if using, with the flour using a large spoon and bring all of the ingredients together to form a smooth, soft dough.

✳ Tip this onto a lightly floured work surface and knead for 5 minutes or until the dough is shiny and free of any floury lumps. Place the dough back into a large bowl and leave it in a warm place, covered with cling film or a clean damp cloth, in a warm place for 1 hour or until the dough has doubled in size.

✳ Once the dough has doubled in size, tip it once again onto a lightly floured work surface and knead it for a minute or two to knock out any large bubbles. Form the dough into a smooth ball and place this, crease down, into the prepared tin.

✳ Cover the dough once again with cling film or a clean damp cloth and allow it to rise for 20–30 minutes until it has doubled in size. While the bun rises for the second time, preheat the oven to 200°C/400°F/gas 6, making sure that there is plenty of space in the centre of the oven for the bun to rise as it bakes.

✳ When the dough is risen, place the cake tin on a baking tray and bake it for 25 minutes, until it is risen and a brown crust has formed. Test the bun by gently tapping the surface to check it sounds hollow.

✻ When cooked, place the bun on a wire rack to cool. For the glaze, place the milk and sugar in a small pan and heat gently to dissolve the sugar. When it simmers, use a clean pastry brush to spread it over the surface of the bun, and as it dries, brush on more glaze until it is all used up. The glaze will dry to a shiny gloss.

✻ When cool, slice the Sally Lunn into horizontal slices, and serve alongside clotted cream and your favourite jam.

· ·

 ## Is a scone a bread, a cake or a biscuit?

The word 'scone' is thought to derive from the Scottish *schoonbrot* or *sconbrot* meaning 'fine white bread'. Traditional Scots scones or 'bannocks' were flat, large and made from unleavened oats, and sharing a cooking technique with flatbreads. They were cooked on a 'girdle' (griddle) in a large round, then cut into pieces before serving. Today they can be made from wheat, barley or oatmeal, but unlike sweet buns, they are leavened with baking powder rather than yeast.

 ## What's the best way to make scones?

Scones are very easy to make but there are several things to watch out for. Firstly, the degree to which the fat and flour are combined will affect the texture of your scones.

If the fat is rubbed in by hand, or blended roughly, the texture of the scones will be coarse. So it's best to use a food processor to blend the flour, sugar and fat together – a very finely blended mixture will give a lighter texture.

However, don't be tempted to use the food processor to mix the milk with the flour and fat mixture. Once wetted, the gluten in the flour can easily be activated in a machine and will result in tough scones. Minimal handling of the mixture is essential for a light, tender scone, so switch to using your more gentle hands at this stage.

Another thing to watch out for is the amount of baking powder you add; baking powder will give a good rise but if you use too much, its flavour will dominate the scone. Self-raising flour is used in the recipe overleaf to avoid this problem, it will still give a good rise to the scones.

You can use strong flour to make scones – the result is a well-risen, light scone – but take care not to overwork the dough as the extra gluten in strong flour can easily be activated, toughening the finished result.

Scones are often served with clotted cream and jam as a 'cream tea'. Although cream teas can be found in most British tearooms, they are frequently associated with the counties of Devon and Cornwall which both have very specific 'rules' as to how to assemble the jam and cream correctly. In Devon, the cream goes on to the scone first, with the jam sitting on top; while in Cornwall the jam is followed by the cream. The debate continues to rage ... For an extra-special homemade treat, why not have a go at making your own clotted cream (see recipe on page 187)?

SCONES

Makes 20 small or 10 large scones
500g self-raising flour
70g caster sugar
125g chilled, slightly salted butter, cut into small cubes
210ml full-fat milk
flour or beaten egg, to finish

1 round cutter, preferably straight-sided – 4–5cms for small scones and 7–8cms for larger; a baking sheet, lined with baking paper

✻ Preheat the oven to 200°C/400°F/gas 6 if making small scones or 180°C/350°F/gas 4 if making large ones.

✻ Put the flour in the bowl of a food processor and add the sugar and butter. Blend until the mixture is very fine and there are no lumps of fat remaining. The mixture should look like a light yellow flour, indicating that the fat is very evenly distributed.

✻ Tip the mixture into a large bowl and make a well in the centre. Add the milk and stir briskly with a fork until the mixture is even – don't try to gather the dough together until it is very evenly blended and there are no lumps of flour present. Once all of the liquid is incorporated, bring the dough together into a smooth, even dough – avoid kneading, which would toughen the scones.

❉ Turn out the dough onto a lightly floured surface and roll out to a thickness of 3–4cm. The way in which you cut out the scones will have an effect on their rising in the oven. A straight-sided cutter, dipped in flour, is best so that the dough is cut smoothly and not compressed, and the sides of each scone are straight.

❉ Once you have cut the scones, place them evenly on the lined baking sheet, spacing them slightly apart to allow for expansion. Pinch together any dough trimmings, trying to avoid incorporating too much extra flour, and re-roll gently to cut more scones.

❉ Dust the scones with a little flour or glaze the tops with a little beaten egg. Bake small scones for 10–12 minutes and large scones for 20 minutes or until they are evenly browned. Cool on a wire rack.

••

PASTRY

Honest, hearty and occasionally a little bit rough around the edges, the versatile pie has provided sustenance for the British for centuries. Although pastry was initially developed for practical reasons – as a means of protecting the food inside it – the use of pastry in British cooking has grown to encompass some of our most iconic bakes, from pork pies and sausage rolls to treacle tarts. Today, pastry-making has progressed from its modest origins to become a highly skilled art form: modern patisserie is a glamorous mixture of elaborate design and creativity with ever more intricate bakes making their appearance on our tea and dessert tables.

Pastry dough is primarily made from fat and flour and by finding out how they interact with each other, you'll be able to appreciate why the fat needs to be kept at a certain temperature and why you shouldn't over-work the flour. Making pastry isn't difficult, but you do need to follow certain rules to avoid under- or over-cooking it, and of course, to avoid every pastry-maker's biggest fear, the soggy bottom. Once you understand the properties of each type of pastry, from the crisp, buttery durable shortcrust to the lighter, flakier types of laminated pastry, you will soon be able to fill them to your heart's content.

EARLY PASTRY

 Who invented pastry?

Given the simplicity of its ingredients it is perhaps no surprise that, like bread, the first documented evidence of pastry-making in Britain dates from Roman times. Roman cookery books, such as *Apicius*, and accounts of feasts by Petronius mention fruit in pastries and egg-shaped pastries each filled with a tiny new-born chick. As butter was not yet available Romans used olive oil or lard as the fat to bind their mixture, but they also devised more delicate sweet pastries, made with honey.

Yet the majority of early savoury pastry wasn't intended to be eaten. Made crudely out of a flour-and-water paste, it was shaped into a covering or case in which to bake food, protecting the contents from the harsh heat of early stoves and ovens, while keeping in the juices. In medieval Britain, stiff pastry cases called 'coffyns' (from the same root as the modern word for funeral caskets) were used to keep food moist while it baked. These encasements were usually made with rye flour and similar in appearance to our hand-raised hot water crust pies, although coffyns weren't normally eaten. Instead, the pastry, once emptied, was used as a thickener in stews, eaten by servants or fed to domestic animals.

When did savoury pastry become an edible delicacy?

It wasn't until the middle of the sixteenth century that the crude flour-and-water pastries began to be enriched with butter and milk, and a version of shortcrust pastry emerged as an edible casing for minced stuffings or small birds. These pie cases were either eaten immediately or, if the cooking juices were drained off and replaced with melted butter or dripping, preserved. The pies could then be kept for weeks and were frequently sent as gifts to friends and relatives.

In 1596 the first recipe for puff pastry appeared in Thomas Dawson's Elizabethan cookbook, *The Good Housewife's Jewel*. It is likely that the method for making puff pastry was already widely known, but this is the first time it appeared in print.

 ## Where did sweet pastry originate?

Lack of written documentation makes it difficult to pinpoint exactly who first feasted on sweet pastries, but it is certain that the Ancient Greeks did: plays written in Greek from around 5 BC mention small fruit-filled pastries.

Evidence of thin, layered baklava and filo pastry can be traced to the southern Mediterranean in the first century and the delicate pastries were brought back to the rest of the Continent by the Crusaders.

By the early-sixteenth century, sweet pastry had become well established and pastries of all description took pride of place on royal tables and in wealthy homes, where they were often extravagantly decorated and gilded. And in northern Europe, from the end of the sixteenth century, small tarts were made with a rich pastry of fine white flour, butter, sugar and saffron. These tarts would have been considered luxury items, not only because of the time taken to make and bake them, pounding the dough into a fine layer before lining the tin, but also because of the quality of the flour and other expensive ingredients they used.

What does 'Viennoiserie' mean?

You may well find references to 'Viennoiserie' in bread-making and patisserie books. The word is French, literally meaning 'things of Vienna', and dates from 1839 when the first Viennese bakery opened in Paris. It refers to sweet, butter-rich pastries made from yeast-risen doughs that are very often laminated like puff pastry. As such, they fall midway between pastry and bread. Danish pastries and croissants are two good examples of Viennoiserie.

THE IMPORTANCE OF FAT

 Can any fat be used for pastry making?

So long as it has a fat content above 80 per cent (check the label), any fat can be used to make pastry, and is interchangeable with other fats with a similar make-up. The results will vary slightly, though, because each fat has a different consistency at room temperature, but as a guide for bakers, the texture of a fat at room temperature is a good clue to the texture of the finished pastry. Fats such as margarines that are quite soft at room temperature will inevitably produce a softer pastry, meaning it will also be more difficult to handle unless it is thoroughly chilled.

Butter, lard, suet, dripping, margarine, oil and vegetable shortenings are all suitable for making pastry. Looking at local pastry recipes from around Europe, we can see that cooks simply used the fat that was most readily available in a particular area.

Of course, the availability of different types of fat depended partly on the landscape of a region. The lush green pastures of southern England, so suited to dairy farming, resulted in local recipes that featured pastry made with cow's butter. By contrast, in southern Europe, where olives are produced in large quantities, you will come across recipes that specify a fruity olive oil for use in pastry. The Spanish *pestinos* is a delicious deep-fried pastry made with olive oil, spices and honey. And in the high mountains of the Alps, where goat herding was more common, butter made with goats' milk was used instead. While cows' and goats' butter can be used interchangeably in recipes, goats' milk will give the pastry a distinct flavour.

The main thing to remember is that the type of fat simply changes the result. Butter, for example, makes the most delicious-tasting pastry, whereas lard, dripping and suet make a light, very short pastry that has a plainer flavour than butter pastry but is crisper and stronger. Olive oil pastry too has a distinctive flavour and is very soft and crumbly and can be quite difficult to handle.

Does the fat content matter?

Fat gives pastry flavour, moistness and richness, but its main job is to interrupt the structure of the flour and water dough to make the baked pastry fragile and tender (crumbly or flaky depending on how the fat is used) rather than hard (think of crackers). While different types of fat (butter, olive oil etc.) affect the final outcome of your pastry, the content of the fat itself also impacts on its texture.

You may be surprised to learn that some fats contain water, but in fact both butter and margarine do and there are set limits for the minimum fat and maximum water content that full-fat butters and margarines must contain: 80 per cent and 16 per cent respectively in the UK.

If a fat contains a lot of water, it will produce a tough pastry because the gluten in the flour is more likely to develop as it comes into contact with the water (see also page 65 for more on gluten and 119 for more on gluten and pastry). For this reason, low-fat margarines (with less than 80 per cent fat) will not make good pastry because the fat has been replaced by water, mixed with chemicals that emulsify the two together.

 Can butter be too old to use?

All fats have a tendency to oxidise when in contact with air, which makes their colour darken and dulls their flavour. In addition, butter contains a small amount of milk sugar (lactose), which can degrade along with other components and turn rancid.

If, when you open a pack of butter and cut into it, the surface is much darker than the interior, the butter is ageing. Waste not, want not – cut away the darker layer and taste the remaining butter. If it tastes OK, it should be fine to use, but for something you plan to eat soon, not a fruit cake that you intend to store for weeks or months.

Unsalted butter ages more quickly than salted because the salt inhibits the growth of microbes. If you come across a good offer on unsalted butter in the shops, buy a quantity and freeze it (cut into 125g pieces) – it will keep for up to 2 months.

What is margarine and why was it invented?

During the 1860s, the rapid industrialization of Europe led to population pressures in growing cities, which began to cause food shortages. In France, Napoleon III offered a reward to anyone who could produce a cheap butter substitute. Money often encourages ingenuity, though not necessarily in the most appetizing ways; early versions blended milk with animal fat, such as dripping, and discarded offal, such as cow's udders, in an attempt to mimic the texture and flavour of real butter.

But in 1869 a French chemist called Hippolyte Mège-Mouriès finally patented the first recognizable version of margarine, made by solidifying meat and vegetable fats, and it began to be produced commercially. Beef fat continued to be used as one of the main ingredients for several decades, however, and it wasn't until the early-twentieth century that the process of hardening vegetable oils by combining them with hydrogen was discovered. Eventually the depression of the 1930s and food shortages of the Second World War caused international problems with the supply of animal fat, and manufacturers began to switch to the entirely vegetable-based products we use today.

Can I use margarine to make pastry?

The degree to which a margarine's vegetable oils are hydrogenated (combined with hydrogen) determines how hard or soft it will be at room temperature. Margarines that are fully hydrogenated are often sold as 'vegetable shortenings' – solid blocks resembling lard or dripping. These contain very little water and behave, in pastry-making, in much the same way as their animal counterparts. If the oils are only partly hydrogenated, however, the fat will be too soft at room temperature and won't be suitable for making pastry.

Lower and very low-fat margarines contain a larger proportion of water, so they behave differently when used in baking and aren't suitable for pastry-making. As margarines have developed, manufacturers have created versions with a similar fat content to butter (80 per cent), mixed with water using emulsifiers such as lecithin. Although this type of margarine can be used for making pastry, its flavour is not as good as butter. If you want to use margarine, always check the label to ensure that it is suitable for baking, and specifically for making pastry.

MAKING PASTRY

 What is the best flour to use for making pastry?

Different types of flour are used for making different pastries – there is no one type that suits them all.

Regular plain flour is best for shortcrust and sweet pastries because of its relatively low proportion of protein (see page 64). As long as you handle your dough delicately, the gluten won't develop elasticity and make the pastry tough. For puff pastry and its relations, however, this very quality – the ability of gluten to develop elasticity – is crucial, so puff pastry is normally made with strong bread flour. This is because the dough has to be rolled very thinly and so needs to be strong enough to avoid tearing. The same is true of filo pastry, which is made by stretching the dough until it is paper-thin.

SHORTCRUST PASTRY

Makes enough to line a 25cm tart or flan tin
250g plain flour
150g slightly salted butter, chilled,
    cut into small cubes
80–100ml cold water

❋ If you are mixing by hand, tip the flour into a large bowl and add the cubes of butter. Using just your fingertips, crumble or 'rub' the butter and flour together until you have a fine breadcrumb-like texture. How finely you mix the butter and flour together will affect the texture of the finished pastry – if you leave the lumps of butter larger, the result will be flakier.

❋ When you are satisfied with the crumb, add 80ml cold water in stages, mixing between each addition so that the butter-flour mix hydrates evenly – this way you are less likely to overwork the pastry than if you add all the water at once. You may need a little more water to bring the dough together, but take care not to add too much as this will make the pastry tough.

❋ Once the dough can be easily brought together with your fingertips, pinch it carefully into a ball, then form it into a smooth, flattened lump. Wrap this in cling film and leave to rest in a cool place or the fridge for a minimum of 15 minutes before rolling out.

❋ To make this pastry in a food processor, pulse the flour and butter together until the mixture resembles fine crumbs. Don't be tempted to add the water to the mixture in the food processor as the machine will easily overwork the dough, making it tough. Instead, tip the crumbs into a large bowl and add the water in stages, mixing each addition in as in stage 2 above.

OLIVE OIL PASTRY

Makes enough to line a 25cm tart or flan tin
250g plain flour
1/2 teaspoon salt
4 tablespoons (60ml) extra virgin olive oil
100–120ml cold water

✳ In a large bowl, mix together the flour and salt. Add the oil and use a large fork to mix the flour and oil together until the oil is evenly incorporated.

✳ Add the water a little at a time, making sure that each addition is evenly incorporated before adding more. When you can pinch the dough together with your fingertips, bring it to a ball and wrap in cling film. Leave it to rest in a cool place for 15 minutes before using.

 What is hot-water crust pastry?

So called because the water and fat mixture has to be heated before it is mixed with the other ingredients, hot-water crust is a fatty pastry, traditionally made with lard. It is also quite a hard and strong pastry that is crisp and water resistant and able to stand up to heavy filling mixtures without collapsing. It is most commonly used for making raised (also known as 'hand-raised') pies, such as pork and game pies.

HOT-WATER CRUST PASTRY

In this recipe, the initial mixing is done with a large fork rather than your hands because of the hot water and lard – so take care. Be sure to have your filling prepared in advance so that the pastry can be filled and topped while still warm, otherwise the pastry won't seal well and the juices from the meat filling will escape.

Makes enough to line a 12-hole deep muffin tin
280g plain flour
1/2 level teaspoon salt
80g lard cut into small chunks
125ml water

✻ Put the flour into a large bowl and stir in the salt.

✻ Place the water and lard in a medium-sized pan and place on a high heat.

✻ When the water and lard mixture comes to the boil, pour it into the flour mixture and stir with a large fork to combine the ingredients together evenly and quickly.

✻ Tip the mixture onto a lightly floured surface and knead briefly until the mixture is thoroughly combined and there are no floury lumps. The pastry is now ready to use.

Do I need to have cold hands to make shortcrust pastry?

The first thing you hear about pastry-making tends to be that cold hands make good pastry. But don't worry, there's no need to stick your fingers in the fridge! The most important thing is to keep the mixture cool as you rub the fat and flour together, which requires the right technique.

Rubbing in by hand will, inevitably, transfer some heat through your fingertips to the fat and cause it to soften. By working quickly and with a light touch, you can minimize the heat you transfer. The best way to keep the mixture cool is to use a food processor. Apart from the heat created by the friction of the blades, the heat transferred to the fat will be minimal. Beware, though – it is very easy to overwork the dough by leaving the machine running for too long.

If the fat does get too warm during the rubbing-in process, you will find you need less water to bring the dough mixture together. Although you might think that this will give you a lovely short pastry, it will most likely mean that the pastry will be too short. It will be dry and crumbly making it tricky to roll out and the baked pastry may fall apart when cut or be cloying in the mouth.

If you think your rubbed-in mixture is too warm or feels tacky, all it not lost. Chill the fat-flour mix in the fridge before tackling the next step of adding water. That way, you will be able to add just enough water to make a perfect dough.

Is it better to make shortcrust pastry in a food processor?

Many experienced pastry chefs use a food processor to make pastry. It is certainly faster than rubbing in by hand, but it can also be easy to overwork the dough so is not necessarily a better method. To prevent this, don't add the water while the machine is running. Instead, once the processor has mixed the butter and flour, tip it into a bowl and gradually mix in the water by hand. This will ensure that you don't add too much water, which would make the pastry tough (see opposite page).

 ## Is it really necessary to chill pastry?

The short answer is yes – and you might need to chill it twice. You should chill pastry before rolling it if you have rubbed the ingredients together by hand or the weather is warm. If the dough feels at all sticky, chill it for half an hour before rolling it out. If, however, the dough isn't sticky or you've mixed the fat and flour together using a machine such as a food processor, you may not need to chill the dough at all before you roll it out.

You will, however, always need to chill the pastry to 'relax, it once it has been rolled out for good reason. Although plain flour contains a relatively small percentage of gluten, what gluten is present can still be activated by the rolling process, causing the dough to become elastic – not ideal when you want to line a tin right to the edge and the elasticity causes the pastry to shrink back as the tart bakes in the oven. By resting the rolled dough in the fridge or a cool place for a few minutes, the stretchy gluten relaxes.

Why does chilled pastry crack when it is rolled out?

Pastry that has been over-chilled will 'set' as the fat solidifies, so when you roll out the flattened lump, the edges will crack. To help prevent this, work the chilled pastry a little with a rolling pin to soften it before rolling out. Place the dough on a lightly floured surface. Sprinkle your rolling pin with flour and hit the dough with short, sharp knocks. The shock waves that run through the pastry will begin to soften the fats and enable the pastry to be rolled out without overworking the gluten. This is less likely to overwork the dough than if you knead it by hand, which could toughen it.

If your pastry continues to crack, it could be a sign that you didn't add enough water to make a pliable dough. To remedy this, chop up the pastry, sprinkle it with a little more water and re-combine into a dough. The end result will require a good deal of resting (a couple of hours), but dry pastry can be salvaged.

Can pastry be frozen?

Absolutely, but you must be sure to use it within a month and thaw it completely before rolling out. Pastry that has no added salt or was made with unsalted butter tends to discolour in the freezer (or fridge) more quickly because it doesn't have the preservative boost of salt. But as long as you use the unsalted pastry within a month, it will still be fine, despite a little discolouration.

If you freeze pastry that's been made with baking powder or self-raising flour, you'll find that it won't have the same texture once thawed and baked. This is because the chemical reaction of the raising agent continues, albeit slowly, in the raw dough as it freezes. The active ingredients will be exhausted by the time the pastry is thawed and baked, so this type of pastry will not tolerate freezing as well.

 ## What sort of pastry should I use for pies or tarts?

You can use any type of pastry for pies, from plain shortcrust and rich shortcrust (with egg yolk added) to rough puff, flaky and puff pastry as well as filo pastry, but you do need to bear in mind how the pastry is being used – whether it needs to hold a filling, or whether it is simply being placed on top as a pie lid.

The challenge with double-crust pies (pies with a top and bottom), quiches and tarts is to make a crust that is sturdy enough to hold the filling without collapsing, but without being tough. A shortcrust pastry is the best suited to this as it's the most robust dough and because you can strengthen it by blind baking (see page 128).

Whatever pastry you use, however, nothing will bake well with a completely liquid filling. The filling will need something, like breadcrumbs, ground almonds or cornflour, to absorb extra liquid as the pie bakes and very wet fillings, such as custard bases, should always be poured into a pastry case that's been baked blind.

A puff pastry is not ideal for a double-crust pie as it is too delicate and wouldn't crisp properly – it needs to be able to expand to let the layers rise, but puff, flaky and rough puff pastry work well as pie lids.

Flaky pastry and rough puff pastry can also be used to make tarts with slightly wet fillings, such as fruit, but they will soak up any excess liquid so need to be baked blind before being filled.

•••

GOOSEBERRY PIE

Serves 8
380g plain flour
190g unsalted butter, chilled, cut into small cubes
130–150ml cold water
1kg gooseberries, washed, topped and tailed

150–180g caster sugar, to taste
1 egg, beaten
2 tablespoons granulated sugar, for glazing

1 x 22–25cm diameter deep pie dish

✽ Make the pastry according to the method for the shortcrust pastry on page 114, and chill for 30 minutes.

✽ Meanwhile, prepare the gooseberries and taste one. If they are very green, you will need to use the larger quantity of caster sugar. If they are beginning to ripen and have a yellow tinge, they will need a little less; some berries won't need any sugar at all.

✽ Preheat the oven to 200°C/400°F/gas 6. Roll out the pastry on a lightly floured board or worktop and cut out a circle just larger than the top of the pie dish – 10cm larger is enough. Using a pastry brush, dampen the edge of the dish with a little beaten egg (egg wash) or water. Cut up the trimmings of pastry and use to line the edge of the dish; moisten this edging.

✽ Pile the gooseberries in the dish and sprinkle with the caster sugar. The fruit will come up higher than the top of the pie dish, but don't worry as it will cook down as it bakes.

✽ Lift the sheet of pastry onto the pie and press the edge to seal to the pastry edging. Using a sharp knife, trim the pastry at the outer rim of the pie dish and pinch to seal. Use any leftover pastry to make leaves or other shapes to decorate the top, sticking them on with egg wash, and cut a small cross in the centre to release steam as the fruit cooks. (Chill the pie now to relax the pastry, if the weather is warm.)

✳ Brush egg wash all over the pastry lid and sprinkle liberally with granulated sugar. Place the pie dish on a preheated baking sheet and bake for 45 minutes. When the time is up, insert a sharp knife into the centre of the pie to check that the fruit is soft.

✳ You could also stir 2 beaten egg yolks into the fruit mixture to thicken the filling.

• •

 ### What's the difference between regular shortcrust and sweet pastry?

The pastry used for tarts and sweet pastries is usually richer and sweeter than that for savoury pies. A sweet pastry is enriched with more butter as well as egg yolks and sugar. A higher percentage of butter doesn't just add to the taste, it also makes the texture shorter and more biscuit-like. Indeed, the French recipe for a *pâte sablée* – the richest of the sweet pastry recipes – is similar to a shortbread biscuit (for more on short pastry and shortbread, see page 56). Egg yolks add a rich gold colour and flavour, while sugar enhances the texture as well as providing a touch of sweetness (caster sugar will make the pastry slightly more crumbly; icing sugar will give a fine-textured, crisper pastry).

PASTRY

Careful, though, a sweet pastry dough needs very careful handling and chilling before rolling out because it contains such a high percentage of fat to flour.

 ## Why is sweet pastry sometimes made using the creaming method?

Sweet pastry is often made by beating or creaming the fat and icing sugar together before adding the egg and then the flour. The pastry is creamed partly to achieve a very fine texture, but also because it is difficult to mix in that much butter by hand while maintaining an even texture to the dough and without overworking it. If the butter is not mixed in well, the baked pastry will be flaky and soft rather than biscuit-like.

• •

SWEET PASTRY

It's easier to make a large batch and freeze half, though you should use this within a month.

Makes enough to line 2x 25cm tart/flan tins
400g unsalted butter, at room temperature
250g icing sugar, sifted
2 egg yolks
2 dessertspoons of white rum or brandy
550g plain flour

✻ Beat together the softened butter and icing sugar in a large bowl until the mixture is well blended and light (do not use an electric mixer – you risk overbeating, resulting in a tough pastry). Add the egg yolk and rum and beat well until they are fully incorporated. Finally, sift the flour into the bowl. Mix thoroughly but do not over beat.

✻ When the dough or paste is thoroughly blended and lump-free, scrape it onto a sheet of cling film and form it into a flattened round. Chill for at least 1 hour before using.

 Why do you sometimes need to roll out pastry between sheets of paper?

Rolling out pastry between sheets of baking paper rather than on a floured surface means that you aren't tempted to add extra flour to your dough. Adding flour at this stage would unbalance your carefully weighed-out proportions of fat to flour and make the texture of your pastry denser and heavier.

This technique is also useful when rolling out sheets of pastry for lining large tart tins – where you need to get the pastry evenly thin – and for handling butter-rich shortcrust and sweet pastry. The paper allows you to work the dough with minimal contact.

TROUBLESHOOTING

 Which are the best tins for tarts and quiches?

When baking pastry it is important that the heat reaches the dough quickly to allow the starch to expand and absorb the fat as it melts. If the starch does not heat up quickly enough, the fat will melt and run out. This loss of the fat will mean that the baked pastry will be tough. The best tins to use are made of either dark metal or glass. Dark metal absorbs the heat of the oven, while glass allows heat to penetrate through, and holds it well once hot. Shiny metal tins reflect away some of the heat of the oven and the dough will take longer to cook.

 Why do you sometimes leave the pastry hanging over the edge when lining a tart tin?

This can help prevent the pastry from shrinking back during baking so that it ends up lower than the rim of the tart tin; any excess pastry can be trimmed level with the tin after baking. This technique also means that you can fill the tart case right to the top.

An alternative is to add a pinch of baking powder to your pastry for each 125g plain flour used. This reduces the likelihood of the pastry collapsing back on itself, however, it also means that the pastry will be more cake-like in texture when baked.

The best thing you can do is make sure you have chilled thoroughly your rolled out pastry to relax the gluten, before baking it (see page 119).

 ## Why do recipes ask you to blind bake pastry?

Baking a pastry case blind will ensure that your pastry is fully cooked, crisp and sturdy enough to hold a filling. You will need some small metallic or ceramic beads known as 'baking beans', but if you don't have them you can use dried pulses, such as lentils, dried peas and beans.

Once you've rolled out the pastry and lined the tin, allow the case to rest in a cool place for 10–15 minutes while you preheat the oven to 220°C/425°F/gas 7 for shortcrust, 200°C/400°F/gas 6 for sweet pastry.

Line the case with baking paper, making sure to press it into the corners. Pour in enough baking beans to cover the base of the case. Bake in the hot oven for 15–20 minutes until the pastry is set and beginning to dry.

Carefully lift out the paper with the beans and pour the beans into a bowl to cool. At this point, you can return the paper to the case and set the round base of a small cake tin on it, which will prevent the pastry from rising. Put the pastry case back in the oven for an additional 15–20 minutes until the pastry is evenly browned. The cake tin base will heat the pastry from above and leave you with a firm, crisp and thoroughly cooked bottom.

If you find the edges are browning a little too much, reduce the oven temperature to 150°C/300°F/gas 2 and allow it to brown through evenly until the base is dry and nicely coloured.

 ## How can I patch up cracks in my tart case?

Chances are we've all had a pastry case that has cracked during baking. There are several reasons this can happen. If your pastry tore as you lined the tart case, it will crack along these lines as it bakes. Cracking can occur because the pastry is too short and has not had enough water added to bind the dough thoroughly. Finally, if you remove the paper lining from a tart case being baked blind, the pastry can crack if it is still a little soft.

The cracking of pastry is annoying, but it is not a major problem. You will no doubt have some pastry trimmings left over, so you can patch up the tart case and return it to the oven. This is best done to a tart case that is almost fully cooked because the firmer pastry will be less likely to crack as you patch it up. While the pastry case is still hot (roughly 10 minutes before the end of the baking time), mould small pieces of raw dough between your fingers and smear it into the cracks. You'll notice that it will begin to melt a little, but as long as you return the tart case to the oven straight away to bake through fully, the cracks will seal. Then you can continue with the recipe and fill the case as usual.

 ## How do I avoid a soggy bottom?

The most effective way of ensuring a pastry case cooks perfectly is to 'blind bake' the pastry case (see page 128), that is, bake the case separately before you add the filling, using baking beans to weigh it down so cooks evenly. Don't skip this important step in a recipe as a 'soggy bottom' can really affect the taste of a tart, pie or quiche. Take heart – it's easily avoided if you prepare your pastry case properly.

Pastry that is undercooked will be raw, grey and soft – a very unappetising soggy bottom indeed. The reason for this is that the pastry has not reached a sufficient temperature during baking to set the starch, and the water has not been driven off. To help prevent this, place your tart tin on a preheated baking stone or a heavy baking sheet, or, if you have a bread oven, place your tart tin on its solid floor. This will get direct heat to the bottom of your pastry case as quickly as possible (see page 127).

Yet, even with a perfectly cooked pastry case, the filling can make the pastry wet and soggy, especially when you've baked a tart in advance that you intend to eat after it has cooled. There are several ways that you can avoid this. The first is to seal – waterproof – the pastry using either beaten egg or melted chocolate. Both work well. Simply brush the egg or melted chocolate onto the baked case and return it to the oven for five minutes until the egg or chocolate has cooked into a shiny layer.

Another sneaky way of limiting this sogginess when making a custard-based quiche or tart, is to part-cook the filling before it goes in – a warm custard filling will set and finish quickly in the oven, resulting in a crisp and delicious base.

'FANCY' TYPES OF PASTRY

 ## What is a laminated pastry dough?

Laminated simply means that layers of fat are created between thin sheets of dough (made with flour, water and fat), which cause the pastry to separate into fine layers when baked. Steam from water in the dough causes the pastry to rise during baking so that the pastry 'puffs up', before the dough sheets set, bake and turn crisp in the final stages of cooking.

There are three types of laminated dough: rough puff, puff and flaky pastry. All three are rolled and folded, to achieve the layering, or lamination, and are best made with a medium to strong bread flour to give the required elasticity to the dough (see pages 64–65). The names puff and flaky are sometimes used interchangeably, so the distinction between them is not always clear, but they are made in slightly different ways (see recipes on pages 136–137), and the technique for rough puff is different again.

There's no getting around it, laminated doughs are time-consuming and quite tricky to make. Mastering the technique of making any of the following doughs will take practice, but as with any type of pastry, the joys of sitting down to a homemade version do make it worth the effort.

What is rough puff pastry?

Rough puff pastry is simpler and faster to make than the other two types of laminated dough, as well as being slightly less rich, but it still has lots of lovely airy layers. It uses the technique of rubbing fat into flour 'roughly' instead of finely, so that large pieces of fat are left in the mixture. After the water is added, the dough is folded and rolled only two or three times.

As it is the simplest of the three doughs to make it's worth giving rough puff a go before trying the other two so that you can get a handle on the folding.

 ## What is puff pastry?

Puff pastry is the hardest of the laminated doughs to make well and is thus rightly considered to be the finest expression of the pastry maker's skill. Although variations of the recipe historically also contain egg yolks, the classic recipe used today has barely changed in the past 100 years – it's that good.

To make puff pastry, a block of fat is positioned on the sheet of dough, which is folded over it. The dough is then rolled and folded up to six times, which results in 700 or so layers being created, all of which puff up as the pastry bakes.

What is flaky pastry?

Flaky pastry is similar to puff but the finished texture is not quite as light and airy as there are not as many layers in the dough. To make flaky pastry, the fat is dotted onto the surface of the sheet of dough, rather than incorporated as a slab. Flaky pastry is easier to make than puff because breaking the fat into flakes and incorporating it into the dough that way is less time-consuming and less complicated than trying to incorporate a large block

ROUGH PUFF PASTRY

Makes 1.3kg
500g strong white flour
500g cold unsalted butter, cut into small cubes
300ml water
1 teaspoon lemon juice

❄ Combine the flour and butter in a large bowl. Using your fingertips, rub the butter and flour together, but stop when only half the butter is incorporated. You should still see large pieces of butter.

❄ Add half the water and stir to a rough mixture, then add the remaining water in batches until you have a dough that will come together easily without being too sticky. Form into a rough ball and turn this out onto a lightly floured worktop.

✻ Roll out the dough, away from you, into a long rectangle 20 x 60cms. Divide it into three sections, marking with a table knife but not cutting it. Fold the top third down over the middle third, then fold the bottom third up over this, creating a square pastry sandwich. Wrap in cling film and chill for 30 minutes.

✻ Place the pastry square on the worktop so that the folded ends are to the left and right. Roll out again into a long rectangle and repeat the folding. Wrap in cling film and chill, then repeat the rolling and folding process once more, to make a total of three times. Wrap and chill the pastry again for at least an hour before using.

· ·

PUFF PASTRY

Makes 1kg
400g strong plain flour
1 tsp fine salt
50g unsalted butter, at room temperature
1 tsp lemon juice
200–250ml cold water
350g unsalted butter, chilled

✿ Place the flour and salt in a large mixing bowl and add 50g butter and rub it into the flour until there are no lumps remaining.

✿ Add the lemon juice to 200ml cold water and add this to the flour mixture in stages, mixing the dough with a large fork. If necessary, add additional water to bring the mixture together to form a smooth, but not sticky, ball of dough. Place the dough in the fridge, wrapped in cling film, to chill and relax for 30 minutes.

✿ Once the dough has rested, prepare the butter slab you are going to incorporate into the dough: sandwich the 350g chilled butter between two sheets of cling film or baking paper on a work surface and, using a rolling pin, beat the butter into a 15cm square. Keep this at cool room temperature while you move onto the next stage.

✿ Scatter your work surface with a little plain flour and place your ball of dough on it. Flatten the ball slightly, and cut a cross in the top. Pull the four flaps of dough apart, flattening them back to form a rough square. Lightly flour the dough and roll it out to a 30–35cm square. Use a pastry brush to remove any excess flour from the surface and place the block of butter on the dough.

✿ Fold the flaps of dough over the block of butter so that it is completely enclosed, making sure that the seams are completely sealed, then turn the dough over. Dust the dough lightly with flour and roll it out into a rectangle approximately 15cm wide and 45cm long.

Divide it into three sections, marking with a table knife but not cutting it. Fold the top third down over the middle third, then fold the bottom third up over this, creating a square pastry sandwich. Wrap in cling film and chill for 30 minutes.

❄ Place the pastry square on the worktop so that the folded ends are to the left and right. Roll out again into a long rectangle and repeat the folding. Chill, then repeat the rolling and folding process a further four times, to make a total of six times. Chill the pastry again for at least an hour before using.

Flaky pastry

Rather than forming a slab of butter as you do for puff pastry, divide the 350g of butter into three equal portions. Once your ball of dough has been made and chilled, roll the dough into a 15 x 45cm rectangle. Divide the dough into three sections and dot one portion of butter (cut into small flakes) onto the top two thirds. Fold the bottom third over the central third and fold the top third back over the central, so that you have three layers of dough and two layers of butter. Chill the dough, wrapped in cling film, for 30 minutes and then roll it out again to another 15 x 45cm rectangle. Dot the butter onto the dough again, roll and fold as before, and chill. Repeat with the final piece of butter. Then, chill the dough for 30 minutes, and repeat the action of rolling the dough and folding a further three times (without butter) to complete the process, chilling for 30 minutes between each rolling.

● ●

I've seen puff pastry recipes referring to 'double-book' folds – what do they mean?

This term describes a method of folding the pastry in between rollings. The puff pastry recipe on page 135 uses a standard technique that gives you three main portions of dough folded over each other. The double-book fold, on the other hand, divides the dough into four portions (without cutting) and folds the outer quarters over the middle two and then sandwiches the middle two together – giving the impression of a closed book.

If using double-book folds rather than the standard technique, the dough is folded and rolled three times rather than six.

 ### Where did the croissant originate?

Despite common assumptions, the croissant is not, in fact, French. Croissant-like pastries were being consumed in Austria long before they appeared in France. According to one legend, the story of the croissant began in Vienna in 1683. Bakers, working through the night, heard digging and Turks were found trying to tunnel under the city wall in an attempt to siege the city. A pastry in the shape of the crescent on the Turkish flag was created to commemorate the event and was named the *kipferl*, meaning crescent. The French version did not arrive in France until the opening of a Viennese bakery in Paris in 1839, which began selling *kipferl*. The French quickly renamed the pastry the 'croissant', also meaning crescent.

Around the turn of the twentieth century, the croissant evolved from the brioche-style dough of the *kipferl* into the light puff pastry we know today.

. . . .

CROISSANTS

This recipe is made over two days. The evening before you bake, make a simple dough and allow it to rise overnight in the fridge. The following morning, layer the dough with butter, then roll, shape and bake.

The temperature at which the croissants prove, or finish rising, is key to their success. A warm room temperature of 23–25°C/73–77°F is ideal: the butter will be soft enough to allow the yeasted dough to rise, but not so warm that it melts out and ruins the recipe. Fast-action yeast is not suitable for this recipe.

Makes 16–18 croissants
1 tablespoon milk powder
250g strong plain flour
250g plain flour
30g caster sugar
10g fine salt
350g unsalted butter
20g fresh or dried yeast, not fast action

300ml cold water

beaten egg, for glazing

2–3 baking sheets, lined with baking paper

❄ Mix together the milk powder, flours, sugar and salt in a large bowl with 50g of the butter, and rub this in until there are no lumps of butter remaining. Cream together the yeast and a little of the cold water in a jug; when it is softened, add the rest of the water. Add to the flour mixture and combine to form a smooth dough – do not knead the dough any more than is necessary to mix it. Cover with a clean cloth and leave at room temperature to rise for 30 minutes.

❄ Punch the dough to knock out any gas, then cover the bowl with cling film. Place in the fridge to rise overnight.

❄ The next morning, shape the remaining 300g butter into a square pat about 2cm thick. Keep the butter at a cool room temperature so it will be easier to roll out.

❄ Remove the dough from the fridge and form into a smooth ball. Set it on a lightly floured worktop. Use a sharp knife to cut a deep cross in the ball. Sprinkle your hands with a little flour, then fold the four flaps of dough outwards to make a rough diamond. Roll out each flap so that the square of butter can be fitted into the centre of the dough. Fold the dough over the butter and seal the edges together with your fingers so that no butter is visible.

❄ Now, you need to roll and fold the dough. Turn the dough over so that the sealed edges are underneath. Using minimal flour, roll out the square of dough away from you into a long rectangle roughly 20 x 60cm. Brush the surface with a pastry brush to remove excess flour, then fold the bottom third of the dough up over the middle third. Fold the top third down so that you now have three layers of dough. Try at all times to ensure that you have a neat, even square. Transfer the dough to a lightly floured tray and chill for 30 minutes to rest.

❄ Repeat the rolling out and folding process two more times, ensuring that you rest the dough thoroughly between each rolling.

❄ Roll out the dough to a rectangle 40 x 75cm. You will find that the dough is very elastic, so allow it time to relax as you roll. Even a rest of 1 minute will enable you to roll the dough thinner.

❄ Trim the edges of the dough rectangle, then cut the sheet in half lengthways to make two long thin rectangles. Brush the dough to remove any excess flour. Cut the rectangles into long triangles, each with a base of about 15cm.

❄ Roll up each triangle from its base towards the tip. Place on the baking sheets and curve the ends inwards to make a crescent shape. Once all the croissants are shaped, allow them to prove for 1 1/2–2 hours at a warm room temperature (do not place them near a direct source of heat or they will rise unevenly and you run the risk of the butter melting out from the dough).

❄ Preheat the oven to 220°C/425°F/gas 7. Bake the croissants for 12–15 minutes until risen and well browned. Cool on a wire rack.

....

 ## What is choux pastry?

Choux pastry is a very light pastry used for making both sweet and savoury concoctions, such as éclairs, profiteroles, choux buns and puffs. It differs from most other pastries because it is cooked twice and is really more of a batter or paste than a dough. The initial cooking occurs when the flour is mixed with boiling water and butter. This creates a partly cooked paste that is then softened by adding eggs. The choux mixture is then piped or spooned into shapes, and once shaped, it is cooked a second time, this time in the oven.

As the choux pastry dough is soft, when it is baked the relatively high proportion of liquid it contains turns the centre of the pastry shape into a steam pocket. As the pastry cooks, steam makes the dough expand to many times its original size. At this stage, the pastry is soft and will collapse easily if the temperature of the dough cools or the pastries are knocked. So don't open the oven door until you can see that the pastry is beginning to brown well and is cooked through. You just have to resist the urge. When baked sufficiently the eggs and fat in the pastry will have set the flour into a crisp, golden case, which is sturdy enough to be filled. If you undercook the pastry it will collapse when it comes out of the oven and turn soggy (see page 130 for how to avoid this).

. . . .

CHOUX PASTRY

Makes 30–40 choux buns suitable for profiteroles
100g unsalted butter, cubed
1/2 teaspoon sugar
150g plain flour, sifted
4 medium eggs (240ml cracked weight)

❋ Combine the butter, sugar and 250ml water in a medium saucepan over a medium heat. Allow the butter to melt, then increase the heat to high and bring the mixture to the boil.

❋ Add the flour to the boiling mixture and draw the pan to one side. Stir with a clean wooden spoon until the flour is fully incorporated. Return the pan to low heat and stir the ball of dough for a couple of minutes so that it dries slightly.

❋ Transfer the dough to the bowl of a large free-standing electric mixer (or, if using a hand-held mixer, place in a large mixing bowl set on a cloth to stop it sliding about). Break the eggs into a separate bowl and beat them together lightly.

❄ Start beating the dough. Add batches of the egg, thoroughly mixing in each addition before adding the next. At this stage, lots of air can be incorporated into the mixture, so don't stint on the beating. When fully mixed, the paste should be glossy and soft enough to just fall from a wooden spoon.

❄ Use immediately, or cover and keep in the fridge for up to 1 day. If you do keep the dough, you may find you have to beat it slightly before using, to make piping easier.

· ·

 ### How can I keep my choux buns crisp?

Of course no one wants a bun that is brittle and hard – but equally you want to avoid one that is too soft to handle once cooked. So how do you achieve that perfect combination of crisp outer edge and soft, doughy inside?

When your choux buns or éclairs are cooked, they still contain a mass of cooked, but wet pastry just under the surface of the crust. The steam trapped inside by the crust will eventually leak out, softening the crust as it does so. You should, therefore, pierce the buns as soon as they come out of the oven. Use a small sharp knife to do this, pricking a hole in the base of each bun – work quickly so you can let most of the steam out before it has a chance to soften the crust – then leave to cool upside down on a wire rack.

If you are going to keep the buns a while before filling them, let them cool completely and keep them in an airtight container. Before you fill them, crisp them up for 5 minutes in an oven preheated to 200°C/400°F/gas 6 before cooling again and filling.

Cooked choux buns can be also frozen successfully for up to one month. Simply thaw the buns, spread out on a baking tray, and crisp up for 5 minutes in an oven preheated to 200°C/400°F/gas 6 before cooling again and filling.

 ## Why do choux buns sometimes topple over when they cook?

Small choux buns may tip over if they are top-heavy. This can occur when the choux pastry is piped – if the mounds of piped dough are higher than they are round, they will be likely to split as they rise and then topple. If the piped mounds are flatter, they are more likely to rise and expand into a perfect round. Don't worry if you are not a perfect piper – once you have piped the dough out on the baking sheets, if any look high, use a wet table knife to press the top to gently flatten the mound and round off the peak.

CHAPTER
FOUR

····················

DESSERTS

When compared with cakes, biscuits, pastries and breads, desserts are fairly recent additions to our recipe repertoire, yet they have become the showstopper finale to a memorable meal.

A trio of simple ingredients – eggs, milk and cream – can be whipped and heated into a glorious alchemy of flavours, but the techniques involved must be applied precisely. Don't be put off – this chapter will show you how to avoid a cracked cheesecake, grainy custard or a collapsing crème caramel. And once you have confidence in whisking egg whites accurately, you can create light-as-air meringues than can be transformed into striking desserts.

The building blocks shared here will give you a base on which to build much more extravagant desserts – just add fruit, chocolate or sauces – until you have created something truly impressive.

THE RISE OF
THE DESSERT

 **When did we start serving a sweet
course at the end of our meals?**

The dessert as we know it is a relatively modern invention.
At the medieval table, sweet items such as dried fruits and
honeyed pastries were eaten alongside savoury foods.

Sugar was still a very expensive commodity during the
sixteenth century and a luxury afforded only by the wealthy.
However, those who could afford to buy it used to show off
by serving 'sweetmeats', such as crystallized or honeyed
fruit, or elaborate sugar or marzipan sculptures placed on
the table at the end of their meal while the dishes were
being cleared. In fact, the word 'dessert' actually derives
from the French *desservir*, which means literally 'un-serve'
or 'clear the table'. And indeed, the practice of serving a
dessert in Britain is understood to have been influenced
by the French. During the early eighteenth century,
the French courts began serving grand and elaborate
pyramids of fruits or sweetmeats as a means of
impressing guests and onlookers with a demonstration
of excess and abundance. Mrs Beeton, writing during the
nineteenth century, also noted that desserts were served
to impress, remarking on the expense of the ingredients,
such as candied fruit and chocolate.

Is there a difference between a 'dessert' and a 'pudding'?

These days, the two words are often used interchangeably to describe the sweet course of a meal and cover a wide range of baked, steamed or boiled and iced dishes. However, they once had slightly different meanings.

Originally, 'dessert' consisted solely of sweetmeats while the word 'pudding' has long been used to describe both sweet and savoury mixtures, including black and white pudding and the Scotch haggis. You can see the connection if you trace the etymology of the word 'pudding' – it came from the Latin *botellus*, meaning 'sausage', which is also the root of the French word *boudin* (a type of blood sausage). These puddings were enclosed in a sausage skin or stomach lining, or even pastry, and baked slowly in a warm oven.

 ## What is a custard?

The word custard derives from the French word *croustade*, which was used to describe an empty pastry case, prior to being filled, most usually with a custard-like mixture, as it is in a quiche. Custard can take many different forms, but at its most basic it is a mixture of eggs and milk which is heated to thicken it.

Understanding custard and, above all, being able to able to make a good custard, is an important skill for any baker as it crops up in so many areas of baking both in savoury and sweet guises.

Custard features heavily in dessert making, where it can be baked to create the dessert itself, as in crème brûlée and crème caramel (see opposite page), or simply used to help build a dessert, as it is in a trifle. Ice creams are very often made with a custard rather than a cream base as the emulsion of eggs and milk is better suited to creating a smooth texture when the mixture is frozen, And in Britain, custard can also be made as a thick or runny sauce to accompany desserts and tarts.

In pastry making, custard is further thickened with flour to make crème patissière (pastry cream), which can be used to fill sweet tarts, éclairs and choux buns or items of viennoiserie (see page 197 for a pastry cream recipe).

And if that weren't enough, we can even use custard to decorate and fill our cakes as the French also created a buttercream out of crème patissière (see page 190 for French buttercream recipe).

CREAMY DESSERTS

 ## What is the difference between crème brûlée and crème caramel?

These are both baked desserts made from custard and caramel, but their flavour, texture and ingredients are subtly different.

Crème brûlée is the epitome of rich baked custards. It consists of sweetened single or double cream thickened with egg yolk that is baked lightly, then cooled and covered with a layer of dark caramel. The caramel may be made separately and poured over the surface or, more traditionally, by melting and caramelizing a layer of sugar directly on the surface of the custard, either by grilling or using a kitchen blowtorch. Once the caramel has set hard, the dessert is chilled briefly before serving.

Crème caramel, on the other hand, is a silky, fine custard made from milk, sugar and whole eggs, or a mixture of whole eggs and yolks. This custard is baked on top of a caramel. During baking the caramel melts and forms a sauce, which flavours and colours the base of the custard. After cooling, the dessert is turned out and served base uppermost, surrounded by the sauce (see page 181 for more on caramel and how to make the sauce).

Egg whites are added to a crème caramel mixture to set it so that the custard can be turned out without collapsing. A custard made with cream and egg yolks, as iin a crème brûlée, is too soft to unmould. If too many egg yolks are added to thicken the mixture, however, they mask the delicate flavour of the cream – it's a tricky balance to get right.

Why are custard desserts baked in a bain marie?

Like many other custard-based desserts, crème brûlée and crème caramel are both baked in a bain marie (a water bath). This technique prevents the custard from getting too hot, as the water acts as an insulating barrier and keeps the custard away from the heat source. If the custard were to get too hot, the water in it would begin to convert to steam, which would cause the custard to rise up like a soufflé and split around the edges. Similarly, if the eggs and milk get too hot, they may curdle.

You don't need any special equipment, a roasting tin with handles at the two ends is a good receptacle to use for your bain marie, so that you risk boiling water sloshing over the edge of the tin and scalding your hands as you transfer the tin in and out of the oven. Place the ramekins or baking dish in the roasting tin and then pour in hot water to come a third of the way up the sides of the dish or dishes (any higher than this and they might float and bump about).

Baked custard recipes will generally suggest cooling

the dish or ramekins on a wire rack. Don't be tempted to skip this as the custard will inevitably continue to cook after it's removed from the oven, but the racks will help to minimize this and prevent your custard from being overcooked.

 ## Why are some cheesecakes baked and others not – what's the difference?

Cheesecakes fall into two main categories: baked and chilled. Baked cheesecakes rely on eggs, or egg yolks, to set the mixture to a rich thick cream, solid enough to be sliced; while chilled cheesecakes usually contain few if any eggs, and are more mousse-like and fresh, using gelatine as a setting agent.

Baked cheesecakes, or tarts, are very common in British baking history. They include the Yorkshire curd tart, a simple, soft fresh curd tart baked in a pastry case and traditionally made with the curds left over from cheese-making.

American cheesecakes derive their thick, rich texture from the sweet creamy cheese used in the filling. If the origins of your cheesecake recipe lie in the Jewish immigrant neighbourhoods of New York, it is likely to use cream cheese as well as soured cream; if it originated in Italian districts, it is more likely to use ricotta. In European-style cheesecakes, lighter cheeses – of varying degrees of ripeness or sharpness – are more often used.

How can I stop my cheesecake's base falling apart?

While traditional cheesecakes were baked either in a pastry case or without any shell whatsoever, in Britain especially, we now tend to use some form of biscuit base. The most common biscuits to use are digestives, which are similar to the Graham crackers often specified in American recipes. These simple biscuits have a relatively unobtrusive taste and so mix easily with any flavour you choose for your filling.

The key to ensuring that your biscuit base does not fall apart is to bake it first, even though it will be baked again with the filling. You should do this even if you are making a chilled cheesecake.

Use biscuits and unsalted butter in a ratio of 2:1. (You can use less butter – as low as 25 per cent of the weight of biscuits – but you'll find that the less you use, the more crumbly the base will be when baked.) Crush your biscuits, either by placing them in a bag and bashing with a rolling pin or by blending them to a fine crumb in a food processor. Mix in melted butter plus some spice or flavouring if you desire – ginger works well for a lemon cheesecake, for example. Spoon the biscuit mixture into a springform tin lined with baking paper and press it down using something flat (e.g. a potato masher or ramekin). Keep pressing until it is even and flat on the base of the tin. Then bake the base to firm it up – 15–20 minutes in an oven preheated to 190°C/375°F/gas 5, until the surface is dry and a shade or two browner.

Remove from the oven and, while it is still hot, carefully compact the base again with your masher or ramekin, as it will have risen slightly as it baked. When cool, you can use this for either a baked or chilled cheesecake and it will give a much firmer and easier-to-cut base.

Why do baked cheesecakes sometimes go grainy and split in the middle?

A baked cheesecake is really only a very thick custard, so like any custard, it can split or go grainy. If overbaked, the edges – and ultimately the centre – of the cheesecake will soufflé (puff up) and coarsen, eventually turning grainy. The centre will probably crack as it cools too.

To avoid cracking and overcooking, bake your cheesecake carefully until the centre reaches 83°C/181°F (the temperature needed to cook custard). Recipes will often tell you to allow baked custards and creams to cook until the edges are set but the centre still has a slight wobble – that is, still a bit undercooked. This is because the centre continues to absorb heat from the base and edges of the mixture after the cheesecake has come out of the oven. Cheesecakes can also split if cooled too quickly, so when its centre is still slightly undercooked, switch off the oven and leave the oven door open slightly to leave it to finish cooking and cool slowly.

Another way to prevent the edges from setting too quickly before the centre is cooked is to bake the cheesecake slowly. An oven temperature of 150–160°C/ 300–325°F/gas 2–3 is sufficient for a small cheesecake (less than 22cm in diameter), while larger ones should be cooked at 140°C/275°F/gas 1. This is because the heat will take longer to penetrate the mixture so the outer portion of the cheesecake will not overcook and go grainy. Heat penetrates the centre of smaller cheesecakes more quickly, so they can be cooked at a slightly higher temperature. The resulting cheesecake will retain a melting texture throughout and shouldn't crack in the centre.

SOUFFLÉS

 Why do soufflés have such a scary reputation?

Baked soufflés are often said to be one of the toughest culinary challenges, and indeed they can be tricky to prepare and bake, not least because they often require the cook to be in the kitchen constantly during the cooking process but they are worth the effort.

Sweet soufflés are made with a custard base (often flavoured with fruit or chocolate) that uses the raising power of egg whites to provide lift and volume. The egg whites expand in the oven, causing the mixture to rise above the level of the dish with a flat, even surface. A soufflé mixture is delicate and light, and can easily be disrupted as it rises by a change in temperature or movement, so be careful at all times and avoid opening the oven while it is baking. Soufflés need to be served and eaten hot as soon as they come out the oven as they quickly deflate!

 Why do baked soufflés stick around the edges?

The shape of the dish and the way it is prepared can affect the way a soufflé rises. A straight-sided dish is best because it allows the mixture to rise evenly with less risk of sticking.

To avoid sticking or an uneven rise, prepare your dish or ramekin carefully. First, use a pastry brush to butter the bottom of the dish, then draw the brush up the sides so that you can see lines of butter (it doesn't have to be a thick layer). Be sure to butter right to the rim of the dish, as this is where soufflés usually stick.

When you have finished buttering the dish, put in some caster sugar and tip and rotate the dish so that the butter is completely covered with a thin layer of sugar. Tip out any excess sugar. Once sugared, the channels of butter will help the soufflé to rise.

Finally, brush a little more butter around the rim of the dish but do not sugar this. Then chill the dishes before filling – this way you won't disrupt the butter layer when you spoon in the soufflé mixture.

You can also run a fingernail or the tip of a knife around the rim of the dish just before baking the soufflé.

Is there any way to rescue a soufflé that is sticking?

The next time you bake a soufflé, observe it in the oven: look at the edge of the dish and, as soon as the surface sets, you will see the mixture begin to mound a little. As the soufflé begins to cook, you should see the mixture rise around the edge. If at any point the mixture is sticking, you have a second or two to open the oven door and quickly run a knife around the stuck mixture. Return the soufflé to the oven immediately.

Your soufflé should still bake perfectly because at this early stage of cooking the main body of the mixture has not begun to heat up. Later in the cooking process, the soufflé would be more likely to collapse if you interfere with it.

 ## Why do some recipes recommend baking soufflés in a bain marie?

This is a good idea when baking small individual soufflés because the heat of the oven can easily penetrate and cook the core of a small soufflé fully before it is properly risen and browned. The bain marie will protect the soufflé from the direct oven heat, allowing the mixture to rise as it cooks.

 ## Can I rebake a soufflé?

As soufflés are very delicate baked desserts, containing little or no flour, they do not like being rebaked. Some soufflé preparations have traditionally been made firmer, however, so that they can be unmoulded and sauced before reheating. Called a *soufflé Suissesse* or a pudding soufflé, these are more frequently made using savoury ingredients. Most soufflé recipes do not contain enough flour to form strong bubbles and, if they are allowed to cool, the bubble walls will collapse and the soufflé won't rise again if you rebake it.

 ## Can I make soufflés in advance?

Most soufflé mixtures can't be kept for anything more than a few minutes before baking because the air bubbles would coalesce, becoming large enough to rise up in the mixture and escape. The soufflés would first coarsen and then fall. If this happens there is nothing you can do.

The one exception to this is a chocolate soufflé where the proportion of chocolate to eggs is 25g chocolate per 60g egg. These mousse-like soufflés will hold because the chocolate sets the bubbles of air incorporated into the mixture along with the egg whites, thus preventing collapse before the soufflé is baked.

Some chefs and writers advocate mixing and freezing soufflés so that they can be baked from frozen. In practice, this can be tricky as the soufflé must be cooked for longer so that it heats thoroughly, otherwise the centre will be cold or even icy. You can, however, prepare the soufflé dishes and base several hours ahead. Then you only have to whisk and incorporate the egg white at the last minute – which won't take much time – and bake. (Note that the base needs to be at room temperature or gently warmed before the egg white is added to it to ensure that the two mix well.)

WHISKING EGGS

 ## What's in an egg white?

Egg white is largely water (90 per cent), with various proteins making up the rest. For convenience you can buy egg white in cartons to use in baking and desserts in place of fresh eggs. As a medium egg white weighs approximately 30g, you can simply convert the number of egg whites you need for a recipe and weigh out the required amount.

Pasteurized egg white, which has been heated to kill off a proportion of any bacteria that may be present, is designed to be used where the white is not cooked – in a mousse, for example.

 ## What happens when egg whites are whisked?

Whisking egg whites breaks down the protein structure so that the protein strands lengthen and air bubbles get trapped inside them. You'll notice that some recipes suggest adding a drop of lemon juice or pinch of cream of tartar before you beat the whites. This is because they help to stabilize the bubbles and the whites will be less likely to go grainy if overbeaten.

Why haven't I been able to whisk my egg whites properly?

You'll see that cookery books tell you to use a scrupulously clean bowl and whisk when making meringues or other recipes containing beaten egg whites, such as soufflés and mousses. There's a good reason for this. Any grease, fat or oil (this includes egg yolk) will stop the egg whites forming a foam. The fat will prevent the protein strands reforming around the air bubbles. So, when separating an egg, make sure that you do not break the yolk into the whites. If you do, remove all specks of yolk before whisking the whites to a foam.

The equipment you use is also crucial to success. Copper or silver bowls have traditionally been used because these metals help to prevent the egg whites from overwhisking. Nowadays, porcelain or glass bowls are more practical and work best because they are easy to clean thoroughly; plastic bowls are often very difficult to get spotlessly clean.

 ## How can you tell if you've underwhisked or overwhisked egg whites?

Underwhisked egg whites will not give you the right volume or texture in your finished bake – but how do you tell and what can you do about it? It's important to look at the texture of the whisked mixture and the peaks that form when you lift out the whisk – these give you the best clue as to the stage the mixture has reached.

When your recipe tells you to whip egg whites to soft peaks, usually needed for soufflés and mousses, watch what happens when you pull the whisk from the bowl – if the whites fall back on themselves and the peaks droop, then you have the soft peaks required. At this stage, the whites will fall out of the bowl if upturned, so it's best not to try this!

For stiff peaks, used for meringues and for piping detailed shapes and baskets, the whites are whisked beyond soft peaks up to the point when they stiffen and form firm, erect peaks when the whisk is pulled out. Egg whites whisked to stiff peaks should not fall out of the bowl when you upturn it – if you dare to try.

If you continue to beat the egg whites beyond this stage, you will overwhisk them: the foam will eventually break down as it first turns grainy and then grey. All is not lost, however, if this happens. You can rescue the whites by covering and chilling them – they will eventually re-liquefy and can be used again, or you can add the same number of egg yolks as whites and use this whole egg mixture for another recipe.

 Who invented meringues?

The first documented recipe appears in 1691 in an influential cookbook *Le Cuisinier Roial et Bourgeois*

by François Massialot, chef to Louis XIV's brother Philippe the Duke of Orléans. Although his recipe coins the name 'meringue', he was not the first to mix egg whites and sugar. English cookery writer Elinor Fettiplace describes a meringue-like white biscuit in her book, *Elizabethan Country House Cooking*, published in 1604.

What is the difference between simple, cooked and Italian meringues?

These three types of meringue are all widely used in desserts and patisserie. Made in different ways, each has its own characteristics.

Simple meringue is the one most commonly used in home baking. The egg whites are whisked to soft peak stage, half the sugar is whisked in, to reach the stiff peak stage, and then the rest of the sugar is folded in. This makes a glossy, firm meringue – suitable for shaped or piped meringues, pies, toppings and pavlova as well as soufflés or mousse – and it must be used straight away otherwise the mixture will re-liquefy.

Italian meringue produces more volume and can be kept for several hours. It's made by whisking the egg whites to the soft peak stage and then slowly whisking in a hot sugar syrup; the heat slightly cooks and stabilizes the whites. This meringue is often used for more elaborately piped desserts, and for petits fours as well as for vacherins and meringue baskets because it keeps its shape well.

Cooked meringue – often called chef's meringue because it's very firm but still flexible and ideal for hot soufflés – is made by whisking the egg whites and sugar in a bowl over hot water to give a huge mass of meringue.

 ### What's the best way to fold whisked egg whites into a meringue mixture or soufflé?

The best tool to use for this is a large metal spoon or spatula because you can use only a few strokes and are, therefore, less likely to overwork and destroy the structure.

Begin by adding a third of the whisked whites to the mixture and incorporate this fully before adding the rest of the egg whites. This will lighten the mixture and make it easier to combine the remaining whites.

 ### Why do my meringues weep liquid after baking?

This happens when the meringue has been over- or underwhisked or when the sugar is not fully dissolved in the egg white, and so the meringue begins to break down almost as soon as it is baked. At first, the mixture will soften and weep a clear liquid; this will, in a few short hours, dissolve the entire meringue.

Weeping is most likely to occur if you have used a balloon whisk or hand-held electric mixer because it's more difficult to dissolve the sugar if the meringue is made in this way. If you have one, it is best to use a table-top mixer to make meringues because it gives the best results. Make sure your egg whites are truly at room temperature before you start whisking, which will help the sugar dissolve fully. Use really fine caster sugar, never granulated, and avoid the coarser kinds of unrefined golden caster sugar, which take longer to dissolve (for more on sugar and its properties and effects in baking, see from page 174).

 ## What is the key to making successful French-style macaroons?

The dainty French-style macaroon biscuits (*macarons*) made from whisked egg whites and almonds are notoriously fiddly to make. Commercial manufacturers use very dry, finely ground almonds to achieve the perfect texture and gloss. This is harder to recreate at home, but you can certainly dry your almonds before you use them, which will give a better texture to your macaroons. Simply spread the ground almonds thinly on clean trays and leave at warm room temperature for a couple of hours before you use them. Sieve the almonds to remove any lumps – the finer the almonds are, the better your macaroons will be.

Getting the meringue component of macaroons right is also very important. As with many recipes, because egg whites from similarly sized eggs can vary a good deal in volume, it's better to weigh the whites to ensure you have the correct amount. And it's vital not to overbeat the whites, so that the macaroon mixture will be soft enough to spread.

Some macaroons are made with simple meringue, while others use Italian meringue. Because Italian meringue is more stable it gives you a little more time to make your macaroons. The recipes below and on page 169 use simple meringue and then Italian meringue to make macaroons – try them both and see what you think.

 ## How do I ensure my macaroons have that lovely glossy flat top?

If you want that characteristic chic, flat top, the trick is to allow your macaroons plenty of time to dry before baking. A 'skin' will form on the surface and, during baking, this will make the interior expand outwards rather than upwards, resulting in a smooth, flat macaroon.

● ●

COCOA MACAROONS

Makes about 30 unfilled shells
120g dried ground almonds (see opposite page
    for how to dry almonds)

170g icing sugar
5 level teaspoons cocoa powder
95g egg whites –
    approximately 3 medium egg whites
pinch of cream of tartar
2 tablespoons caster sugar

1 piping bag, fitted with a 10–12mm plain nozzle;
3 baking sheets, lined with baking paper

❋ Sift together the ground almonds, icing sugar and cocoa twice, to combine evenly. Discard any large pieces of almond that remain.

❋ Put the egg whites in a large bowl, add the cream of tartar and beat using a hand whisk for 20 strokes until they are just frothy. Add the caster sugar and continue to whisk until you have soft peaks. Tip in the almond mixture and fold in gently using a large metal spoon.

❋ Transfer the mixture to the piping bag. Pipe flat discs of mixture approximately 2.5–3cm in diameter onto the lined baking sheets, spacing them 1cm apart. Lightly bang the sheet on your worksurface to flatten the macaroons a little. Set the baking sheets in a warm dry place and leave until the surface of each macaroon has a dry 'skin' (see page 167). This can take between 30 minutes and 1½ hours, depending on the relative humidity of your kitchen. Keep checking using your fingertip – if it sticks to the macaroons, they are not ready.

❄ When the macaroons have set, preheat the oven to 150°C/300°F/gas 2. Bake for 18 minutes in a conventional oven. If using a fan oven, bake for 15 minutes until the meringues are risen and a shade darker.

❄ Remove the baking sheets from the oven and allow the macaroons to cool for 15 minutes before removing them from the sheets to a wire rack. Leave to cool fully before sandwiching with either a fruit preserve or a flavoured buttercream.

The macaroons can be kept unfilled in an airtight box, layered between sheets of baking paper, for up to 2 days.

ITALIAN MERINGUE MACAROONS

Makes about 45 unfilled shells

200g dried ground almonds
(see page 166 for how to dry almonds)
200g icing sugar
150g egg whites – approximately 5 medium egg whites
pinch of cream of tartar
200g caster sugar
50ml cold water
2–3 drops edible food colouring of your choice (optional)

1 temperature probe or sugar thermometer; 1 piping bag, fitted with a 10–12mm plain nozzle; 3 baking sheets, lined with baking paper

❄ Sift together the almonds and the icing sugar twice. Discard any large pieces of almond that remain. Mix half (75g) the egg whites into the almond mixture.

❄ Put the remaining egg whites and cream of tartar in the bowl of a large, free-standing electric mixer. Turn it on to beat slowly so that the egg whites gradually begin to thicken and then form soft peaks.

❄ Meanwhile, put the caster sugar in a small saucepan and moisten it with the water. Place on high heat and allow the sugar to dissolve without stirring. Then bring to the boil and simmer for 2 minutes. Now test the temperature of the sugar syrup with the probe (or thermometer). When the syrup reaches 118°C/245°F, remove from the heat and pour it in a steady stream onto the egg whites while they are still beating.

❄ Allow the meringue to continue beating gently until it cools, adding any colouring you want to use when the meringue is cold, ensuring that it is evenly blended.

❄ Add the almond mixture and fold in gently using a large metal spoon. Stir until it is soft enough to flow gently from the spoon, then transfer to the piping bag. Pipe discs approximately 2–3cm in diameter onto the lined baking sheets, spacing them 1cm apart. Gently bang each baking sheet a few times on your worksurface to make the macaroons flatten a little.

❋ Leave the macaroons at warm room temperature to set and form a 'skin' (see page 167) – this will take between 30 minutes and 1 ½ hours, depending on the humidity of your kitchen. Once they have, preheat the oven to 150°C/300°F/gas 2 and bake the macaroons for 18 minutes in a conventional oven and 15 minutes in a fan oven. The macaroons are ready when they have risen and a shade darker.

❋ Remove from the oven and leave to cool for 10 minutes on the baking sheets before transferring to a wire rack. Cool completely before sandwiching. The macaroons can be kept unfilled in an airtight box, layered between sheets of baking paper, for up to 2 days.

CHAPTER FIVE

FLAVOURS
AND
FILLINGS

In this last chapter, we focus on the key, classic ingredients: sugar, cream, vanilla and chocolate. Where would the baker be without them?

These ingredients will transform a bake, bringing flavour and texture, richness and aroma to your recipe. Think of how dull a choux bun would be, without a cream filling and chocolate topping, and how it is transformed into an elegant croquembouche with the small additions of caramel and vanilla cream. Sugar may be a basic baking ingredient now, but for many centuries honey was the only sweet flavouring (other than fruit) available to British bakers. Yet from the late-fifteenth century sugar transformed European baking into an elaborate and elegant art form, as bakers realized its full potential in crystal and melted form.

Cream, too, has the power to enhance both sweet and savoury cooking, providing it with a touch of luxury. The simple act of whipping cream can completely change its form and opens up an array of ways to use it; from sandwiching a sponge cake and filling a roulade, to combining it with chocolate to make a luxurious ganache.

Chocolate is, of course, a vital and increasingly popular ingredient in baking but it does need to be handled with care. By finding out where chocolate comes from, how it is produced and what makes up the properties of the different types of chocolate available, you'll understand how best to use it in your bakes to make them as delicious as the bar itself.

SUGAR

What exactly is sugar?

Sugar occurs in all living things and is essential to the nutrition of plants and animals, including humans. It is a form of carbohydrate so provides us with energy.

Of the many different forms of sugar, the most basic are glucose and fructose. Both are simple sugars, or monosaccharides, which means they cannot be broken down any further by hydrolysis (reacting with water).

Disaccharide sugars contain two monosaccharide sugars. Our familiar granulated white sugar is a disaccharide sugar made from one glucose and one fructose molecule.

The different mono- and disaccharide sugars vary in sweetness because of how our taste buds respond to the particular shape of the molecules. If you were to taste the various forms of sugar one after another, you would understand how remarkably different they are.

How is sugar made?

The familiar types of sugar we use in our cooking are extracted from the sap of two plants: a giant grass (sugar cane) and a root (sugar beet). In order to extract the sap, the cane or beet is shredded and then pressed, or spun in a centrifuge, to squeeze out the juice. This juice was once boiled in large vats, but these days it is processed in a vacuum chambers, boiled and evaporated to concentrate it and produce a sugar syrup. Some sugar crystals are then added to the syrup to 'seed' the mixture, which encourages more sugar crystals to form. As they form, some or all of the residual liquid (known as molasses) is drawn off. The remaining mass of sugar crystals is then blow dried with hot air. The sugar can then either be left as it is, as a brown unrefined sugar, or further refined (see next question).

 ## What is the difference between unrefined and refined sugar?

Raw, or unrefined, sugar is a naturally light brown sugar that has undergone the minimum of processing. The colour and the type of unrefined sugar depends on the amount of molasses that has been removed. Types of raw sugars include Demerara, molasses and Muscovado (see next question for more information on these). Be aware that sugars that are labelled as 'brown sugar' are actually refined white sugars that have had varying degrees of molasses added back into them to colour them and make them look either light or dark brown. Unrefined brown sugars will add additional caramel flavour to a bake and, depending on how rich in molasses they are, they will also make the bake more fudgy in texture. Unrefined sugars also dissolve more slowly than refined and contain more moisture, which is good for fruit cakes and gingerbread; less so for pastries.

Refined, brilliant-white sugar is created by bubbling sulphur dioxide gas through the initial mixture of cane or beet juice, which bleaches it and removes all the colour.

What do the names of the different types of sugar mean?

Cane sugars were often named after the place where they were first produced: Demerara sugar was originally made in Demerara, a region in what is now Guyana, South America, which was one of the earliest Dutch colonies in the Caribbean; Barbados sugar, also a brown sugar, was made by the Dutch from 1700, taking over from cotton and tobacco as the main industry of the island.

Demerara sugar crystals are hard, large and light brown in colour with a rich aroma. Demerara gives an excellent, crunchy topping to cakes and muffins, sprinkled on top of the mixture before it is baked because the size of the crystals prevents the sugar from melting.

Barbados sugar, also sometimes called molasses sugar, is the coarsest and darkest of the unrefined sugars, with a sticky quality that makes it excellent for making gingerbread and dark fruit cakes.

Muscovado is a similarly dark unrefined sugar, which some argue derives its name from the Spanish for, 'more finished', suggesting that the sugar is slightly more refined than Barbados sugar. Muscovado is available in dark and light forms according to the amount of molasses each contains (dark is about 13 per cent molasses and light about 6 per cent). The dark form has the richest taste and strongest aroma and, like molasses sugar, is used in darker fruit cakes and puddings.

 ## Does sugar go off?

If kept in an airtight container, sugar will keep indefinitely. Unrefined sugars, if not kept airtight, will solidify into one hard block or large lumps. This is because the moisture they contain evaporates. To rescue a brick of sugar, put it in a bowl, cover with a damp tea towel and leave it overnight.

 ## What is caramel?

Caramel is melted and browned sugar. But while sugar can be heated in a dry pan to melt it, it is more often dissolved in water first to make caramel. Dissolving the sugar in water means that the melted sugar can be subjected to greater temperatures.

Sugar syrup passes through different stages during heating on its way to becoming caramel and each occurs within a specific temperature range. These stages of sugar syrup have different uses, as shown in the table below.

When the sugar dissolves and the syrup boils the water evaporates. The more the water is evaporated, the greater the concentration of sugar and the thicker the syrup becomes, until it reaches saturation point. The more concentrated the syrup, the less moisture it will have, which means it will set harder.

Temperature	Stage of sugar	Concentration
110–113°C/ 230–235°F	thread stage	80 per cent (used for simple fudges, iced parfaits and Italian meringue)
113–116°C/ 235–241°F	soft-ball stage	85 per cent (used for fruit gums and nougat)
118–121°C/ 244–250°F	firm-ball stage	87 per cent (used for softer toffee and caramel)
121–129°C/ 250–264°F	hard-ball stage	92 per cent (used for harder toffee and caramel)

132–143°C/ 270–289°F	soft-crack stage	95 per cent (used for butterscotch and brittles)
149–154°C/ 300–309°F	hard-crack stage	99 per cent (used for honeycomb and fruit toffees)
155–165°C/ 311–329°F	caramel	99–100 per cent (used for spun sugar and caramel syrups)

A sugar thermometer will help you to make sure you take the pan off the heat at the correct moment. Once the caramel reaches your desired temperature, dip the base of the pan into cold water to stop the caramel overheating.

 Why does caramel sometimes go grainy?

If you make a concentrated sugar syrup you might notice that, as the water begins to evaporate from the edge, small crystals of sugar start to appear. This is because when a crystalline substance like sugar is dissolved and then concentrated it can quite easily turn back into crystalline form. Transparent sheets of sugar crystals can also appear on the surface, rather like ice that forms on a frozen pond.

The graininess is less likely to occur if you are using a gas hob because the gas flame usually heats the outside of the pan as the flame licks up the sides, melting any crystals of sugar that may start to form at the edge.

There are two ways to lessen the risk of your caramel becoming 'grainy'. First, make sure that you dissolve the sugar completely in the water before beginning the process of heating it to a caramel. Second, carefully wash down the interior of the pan with clean boiling water as the caramel cooks, using a clean pastry brush. Any crystals that do form will be dissolved and absorbed back into the boiling syrup.

Most importantly, do not stir the caramel as it cooks because this will encourage the syrup that collects on the sides of the pan to crystallize. Some chefs add golden syrup to the sugar syrup in order to help guard against crystallization, and also to produce a more flexible caramel (see also page 182 for info on golden syrup used spun sugar).

 ## What is meant by the terms 'dry' and 'wet' caramel?

To make a hard or 'dry' caramel, sugar syrup is heated to a high temperature then allowed to cool and harden to a brittle, glassy substance used for creating spun sugar and pralines, among other things.

If you want to make a 'wet' caramel that can be used for making crème caramel or caramel sauce, for example, you need to add some water to the hot caramel. Take great care when doing this! First, remove the pan from the heat and dip its base in a tub of cold water – this will stop the caramel cooking immediately and prevent it burning. Then, carefully add a small quantity of boiling water to the pan – say 100ml for every 200g of sugar used in the recipe. Cover your hand with an oven glove and stand back as the mixture will splutter and the pan will hiss with steam. Then return the pan to a gentle heat to allow the caramel to dissolve, and simmer to your desired consistency, be it a light syrup for soaking sliced oranges in or a thick syrup for serving alongside a baked cream.

 ## What's the best way to make a caramel for crème caramel?

A thick 'wet' caramel syrup that will remain liquid when the custard is added is a good choice. As long as the syrup is dense enough, the custard will float on top of it and bake perfectly. The caramel sauce will have a pourable texture when the cold custard is turned out of its mould.

To make a thick caramel syrup, combine 160g granulated sugar and 6 tablespoons of water in a clean stainless-steel pan (not a non-stick pan, which would cause the syrup to crystallize). Dissolve the sugar slowly over a low heat, stirring with a wooden spoon. When there are no sugar granules left, stop stirring and bring to the boil. Boil rapidly for a few minutes until the sugar turns a dark caramel colour. Remove from the heat and dip the pan's base in a bowl of cold water to prevent the caramel overcooking and burning.

 ## Is there a trick to making caramel for spun sugar?

Mixing in a little golden syrup with the sugar and water makes a flexible caramel that seems to be more stable for longer. Simply add 1 tablespoon of golden syrup for each 100g caster sugar in your recipe then make the caramel as usual.

 ## What is praline?

Popular for centuries in France, praline was originally a sweet made by coating whole almonds in grainy caramel. Today it can describe any mixture of nuts (though it is still most usually almonds) cooked in clear caramel, then cooled. Once set hard, the praline is either ground and added to sweet dishes or broken into pieces for use as a decoration.

Can I substitute honey for sugar in baking?

Yes, you can, but there are three things you need to bear in mind. First, honey comes in a variety of flavours, ranging from very bland and merely subtle, to very strong and overwhelming, so when choosing a honey you need to be sure you choose a mild kind and be prepared for your bake to taste of it! Stronger-flavoured honey can work well with chocolate and cinnamon, and in apple and other fruited cakes, but you should use a mild honey to blend with vanilla.

Honey will also add more sweetness to a recipe because it's sweeter than sugar. A good rule of thumb is to use three-quarters of honey for the amount of sugar given – so 75g honey for each 100g sugar.

It contains around 15–20 per cent water, so if your recipe contains additional liquid, such as milk, then you need to reduce the quantity of liquid by 20 per cent. If there is no additional liquid in the recipe, such as in a sponge, honey will make a less fine sponge because of its extra water content, but the recipe will still work.

 ## How is maple syrup made?

Like cane sugar, maple syrup is extracted from the sap of a plant – in this case a maple tree, *Acer saccharum* – and then boiled to concentrate it. But unlike cane sugar, the resulting maple syrup is not greatly refined.

The indigenous peoples of North America discovered the technique of bleeding maple sap from the tree. Records dating to 1600 from the Great Lakes region show the trade in maple syrup and maple sugar between the settlers and native Indian tribes.

All tree sap contains some sugars, dissolved so that they can be more easily transported around the plant. To extract the sap, a small number of holes are bored in the trunk of a tree once it has reached a certain size and age – when it is about 40 years old. At any time during the dormant winter season, the sap rises in the tree and then starts to emerge from the holes in early spring, to be collected through pipes. Sap collected later in the season is lower in sugar content, and has to be boiled for longer to concentrate it, so is darker in colour with a stronger flavour.

Maple syrups are graded according to their strength. Grade I is the lightest, with the most delicate flavour. Grade II is darker and better for baking as it has a stronger flavour.

CREAM AND BUTTERCREAM

 What is the difference between the various types of cream?

In the UK, you can buy several types of fresh cream that differ in their minimum fat content:

Cream type	Butter-fat content
Half cream	12 per cent
Single cream	18 per cent
Soured cream	18 per cent
Whipping cream	35 per cent
Crème fraîche	35 per cent
Double cream	48 per cent
Clotted cream	55 per cent

There are also lower fat versions available but they generally aren't suitable for use in baking as they are often thickened with gums and react differently to being heated.

Cream in other countries also varies – in both name and fat content – so be sure to check carefully if you are following an American or French recipe, for example.

What is clotted cream?

Thick and rich, this decadent cream is made by gently heating milk and cream together in a large shallow pan. When the cream rises it forms the 'crust' – a slightly firm thick yellow layer that is characteristic in clotted cream – which is then skimmed off using a shallow ladle and set in trays. Usually the cream is 'ripened' at room temperature overnight before being skimmed to allow a deeper, richer flavour to develop. Clotted cream is made across the UK, but we tend to associate it with the south-west of England, where Cornish Clotted Cream has been awarded a PDO by the European Union. (PDO means Product of Designated Origin, and is a legal status given to specific products within the EU that have a clearly identifiable historic and regional basis.) Cornish Clotted Cream must be made to certain guidelines and use only Cornish milk. Clotted cream can be made elsewhere, but cannot be labelled as Cornish Clotted Cream.

You can make your own clotted cream using the recipe opposite and then serve it with some homemade scones (see page 102) or a slice of Sally Lunn bun (see page 98). The richer the milk and cream you start with, the better – Jersey or Guernsey milk and cream will give you the highest yield.

CLOTTED CREAM

Makes 250–300g
600ml double cream
300ml milk

✳️ Combine the cream and milk in a large, shallow non-reactive pan, such as stainless steel, and cover with a clean cloth. Leave at room temperature overnight.

✳️ The next day, set the pan on the lowest possible heat. Do not stir.

✳️ After about 1 hour, cream will begin to rise to the surface. As it starts to solidify, use a large spoon or shallow ladle to skim the cream off the top. Transfer it to a shallow dish, keeping the 'skin' uppermost (this is the key to developing the yellow-crusted surface that is essential for clotted cream).

✳️ Continue to skim off the cream as it rises. Eventually you will have skimmed all the fat from the mixture. Allow the cream you have collected to set overnight in the fridge, covered with cling film. This can be stored for up to five days.

 What is crème fraîche?

Crème fraîche is made by adding a bacterial culture to cream and leaving it to sour and thicken. Unlike a cream

FLAVOURS and FILLINGS

cheese, it usually isn't strained, so its water content is higher than cream cheese, and the mixture is lighter and more fluid.

You can make your own crème fraîche at home, using a powdered yoghurt culture, which is available from health food shops or smallholding suppliers. Or you can use live plain yoghurt, available in most supermarkets, which has the same bacteria that are present in the powdered culture.

To make crème fraîche with live yoghurt, first heat some double cream to 32°C/90°F over a medium heat, then pour into a glass or stainless steel bowl. Stir in the live yoghurt in the ratio of one part yoghurt for three parts cream. Leave the mixture at room temperature, covered with a cloth, overnight, and then refrigerate for up to five days.

 ## Can I use crème fraîche in place of cream?

Crème fraîche has different properties to cream, so you won't be able to use it to replace cream in most baking recipes. The one exception is that full-fat crème fraîche can be used in place of whipped cream. However, crème fraîche should not be whipped because it can't retain air as cream does when whipped, and so will become more liquefied, not thicker. Any mixture you make with crème fraîche will, therefore, be denser.

You can, of course, substitute crème fraîche for soured cream in fillings and toppings or in cake mixtures, where its mild acidity will work just as well.

 ## What is butter icing?

A butter icing is a very simple, quick icing made from beaten butter and icing sugar. It can contain added milk to give a looser, creamier texture, plus flavourings. Used to sandwich and top sponges and fairy cakes, butter icing is much thicker and not as creamy as buttercream, but is a handy recipe to have on standby if you need to finish a cake in a hurry.

To ice 24 fairy cakes or 12 cupcakes, or to sandwich and top one 20cm sponge cake, beat 125g unsalted butter with 400g sifted icing sugar and 3–4 tablespoons of milk.

 ## Why do recipes for buttercream vary – isn't it a simple formula?

Not to be confused with butter icing, a classic British buttercream is made from unsalted butter, icing sugar and egg yolks. The sugar is melted with water and then boiled until it reaches 110°C/225°F (you'll need a sugar thermometer to get this right). The hot sugar syrup is poured over beaten egg yolks, in a steady stream, while the mixture is whisked. This thick, mousse-like mix, now pale and cold, is whisked with the butter and any flavourings to create the buttercream.

There are many versions of buttercream, including French and Italian meringue buttercreams, which are slightly trickier to make than British buttercream. These recipes use a cooked base – a thickened milk custard, like crème patissière, in the case of French buttercream. For an Italian meringue buttercream, an Italian meringue beaten with unsalted butter.

· ·

FRENCH VANILLA BUTTERCREAM

Makes approximately 550g
250ml full-fat milk
125g caster sugar
1 vanilla pod, split
25g cornflour
250g unsalted butter, at room temperature

❁ Place 4 tablespoons of the milk in a medium bowl and set to one side. Pour the remaining milk into a medium saucepan set over a medium heat and add the caster sugar and vanilla pod. Heat the mixture until it begins to steam, then leave to infuse off the heat for 10 minutes.

❁ Remove the vanilla pod, scraping the seeds into the pan (if you wash and dry the pod you can place it in a jar of caster sugar to flavour the sugar – see page 196). Put the pan of flavoured milk back on the heat and bring to a gentle simmer.

✳ Meanwhile, mix the cornflour with the reserved cold milk. When the flavoured milk simmers, pour it onto the cornflour mixture and stir to combine. Return the mixture to the pan and simmer over low heat for 2–3 minutes so that the cornflour cooks through, stirring constantly.

✳ Remove the pan from the heat and pour the mixture into a clean bowl. Place a clean cloth over the bowl to prevent a skin from forming, then leave to cool completely.

✳ Beat the cold vanilla mixture to lighten it, then sieve to remove any lumps. In a separate bowl, beat the soft butter to lighten it. Add the vanilla mixture in small quantities, beating well with each addition. The buttercream can now be used.

• •

ITALIAN MERINGUE BUTTERCREAM

This recipe does make a large quantity of buttercream, but it is hard to divide some of the ingredients into smaller quantities. If you want to make less, make the full quantity of meringue, but use half the meringue for another recipe and then reduce the butter quantity by half.

Makes approximately 675g
3 medium egg whites, at room temperature

225g caster sugar
4 tablespoons water
20g liquid glucose
375g unsalted butter, at room temperature
seeds from 2 vanilla pods or 50g dark chocolate,
   melted and cooled

❇ First, put the egg whites in the bowl of a large, free-standing electric mixer.

❇ Combine the caster sugar, water and glucose in a small pan and allow the water to soften the sugar for a few minutes. Then place the pan on a medium heat and allow the sugar to dissolve without stirring. Occasionally moisten the inside of the pan using a clean, wetted pastry brush to prevent the sugar from re-crystallizing. Bring the syrup to a simmer and cook until it reaches 110°C/230°F on a sugar thermometer.

❇ Now turn on the mixer and beat the egg whites to soft peaks. When the syrup reaches 120°C/248°F, remove the pan from the heat and pour onto the egg whites in a constant stream, beating slowly but continuously. Beat the meringue for a few more minutes until it is cool.

❇ To finish the buttercream, beat the soft butter in a large bowl to lighten it. Beat in the vanilla seeds or chocolate, then gradually beat in the meringue mixture. The buttercream is now ready to use.

What is the difference between glacé icing, royal icing and fondant icing?

All three icings are essentially made from icing sugar and water, but by employing varying methods and additional ingredients they can be used to create very different effects.

Glacé icing is the most basic of the three and is made from sifted icing sugar mixed with a liquid – usually water, orange or lemon juice. For a smooth icing that can be piped, mix 100g icing sugar with 2 ½ teaspoons of water or juice. Add more liquid, a few drops at a time, if you want a runny icing that can be drizzled. It will firm up a little as it dries but will not harden completely. You can use glacé icing to ice fairy cakes or as a quick decoration for biscuits and fruit cakes.

Royal icing is a more robust option, made from icing sugar beaten with egg whites and lemon juice, which sets to a hard finish once dried. If you want to avoid using raw egg whites, you can use royal icing sugar instead. This contains dried egg whites. Royal icing can be used to cover cakes, for piping work and for decorating biscuits. You can control how hard your royal icing will set by adding a little glycerine: ½ teaspoon of glycerine per 500g icing sugar will create an icing that can be used to cover a cake but it won't be rock hard.

Fondant icing is made from icing sugar, water and liquid glucose, mixed to a soft dough that can be rolled out to cover a cake or make decorations. You can buy it ready-made, or you buy fondant icing sugar, which is made from icing sugar and dried glucose syrup. Mixed with water or juice it makes a glossy, satin icing that is more substantial than glacé icing and can be used to coat cakes or be made into modelling paste for sugar craft. Blocks of fondant modelling icing, also called ready-roll or sugar-paste icing, are now widely available to buy in a range of colours.

VANILLA

 Why is vanilla such a luxury ingredient?

Seed-filled vanilla pods come from an orchid, *Vanilla planifolia*, that originates in the tropics of Central America and has been used for centuries to provide seductive sweet and spicy flavouring. The Aztecs had been flavouring their chocolate drinks with vanilla long before the first Europeans arrived in the 1500s and took up the idea. Interestingly, although vanilla itself is bitter, it is always associated with sweet foods.

In its natural habitat, the orchid flowers are pollinated by a particular species of Mexican bee. The first attempts to cultivate the plants outside of Mexico failed, until it was discovered that the flowers could be pollinated by hand using a pointed stick or blade of grass. That is pretty much how it is still done today.

Once the flowers are pollinated and the pods have appeared, these are harvested and fermented, which takes a number of months. This whole process is labour-intensive and time-consuming, which explains why vanilla pods are so expensive.

What is the difference between vanilla essence and extract?

The substance that gives vanilla its beautiful taste is called vanillin. This can be extracted from vanilla pods or it can be made artificially.

If it has been extracted from a natural source, it will be labelled 'natural' vanilla flavouring or extract.

Synthetic vanillin, as with other artificially created flavourings, is made into essence and by law has to be labelled as such. Synthetic vanilla flavouring lacks the depth of vanilla extract or vanilla pods, but it is cheaper to buy.

Vanilla paste, which is the scraped-out inside of a vanilla pod, is another good option.

 ## Can I reuse vanilla pods?

Yes, but not in the same way. Once you have used a vanilla pod to flavour, say, a custard, rinse it well to remove all traces of dairy products or eggs. Then dry it thoroughly on clean kitchen paper in a low oven for 1–2 hours. Push the pod into a jar containing caster sugar, so that the sugar can absorb the subtle vanilla flavours.

You can then use the vanilla sugar to replace plain caster sugar in all kinds of baking and other sweet cookery. One particularly delicious use for vanilla sugar is in pastry cream (see opposite page).

What is the difference between pastry cream and crème anglaise?

Both of these are custards made with eggs and milk, flavoured in the same ways – most commonly with vanilla or chocolate – but their ingredients and uses are quite different. Pastry cream, also called crème patissière, is a sweetened mixture of milk and eggs that is stiffened with a little flour. Crème anglaise (the posh term for a proper egg custard) is a richer mixture of egg yolks, usually made with single cream and milk; it doesn't contain any flour so has a pourable consistency. The thicker pastry cream is used as a filling, for all sorts of cakes, tarts and pastries such as choux buns or éclairs, whereas crème anglaise is served as a sauce – normally, but not always, chilled – to accompany desserts.

··

PASTRY CREAM

The combination of plain and corn flour used here, gives a lighter texture to the finished pastry cream than if you had used plain flour only.

Makes approximately 650ml
500ml full-fat milk
125g vanilla sugar
1 vanilla pod, split in half lengthways
6 egg yolks
20g plain flour
20g cornflour

✿ First, infuse the milk with vanilla. Place the milk, half the sugar and the vanilla pod in a medium saucepan set over low heat and heat gently until the milk begins to steam. Set aside for 10 minutes.

✿ Meanwhile, mix the egg yolks with the remaining sugar in a medium bowl and beat well until the mixture is light. Sift in the flour and stir well so that there are no lumps.

✿ When the milk has infused, strain it through a sieve into a clean pan and heat over medium heat until it begins to simmer. Pour the hot milk over the egg mixture, whisking to combine them well.

✿ Pour back into the pan and bring to a simmer, stirring all the time with a clean wooden spoon. The cream then needs to boil for 2–3 minutes to thicken and lose any taste of the flour. Transfer to a clean bowl and leave to cool completely before refrigerating. Use the cream when cold, beating to loosen it a little. You can store this in the fridge for up to 4 days, keeping the cream well covered at all times so it does not absorb any flavours.

•••

 Why does pastry cream liquefy?

If pastry cream is not fully cooked it will collapse – sometimes with disastrous effect. The egg yolks in the mix contain an enzyme that can liquefy the cream, so it is essential to cook it sufficiently as heating the enzyme changes its shape and thus its properties, making the pastry cream more stable. Boiling it for 2–3 minutes should do the trick.

. . . .

CRÈME ANGLAISE

The method described here is slightly different to the one generally used for making custards. It is included because it is faster: heating the flavoured milk and cream mixture to a simmer and then pouring it onto the egg yolks while stirring instantly cooks the yolks and thickens the custard.

Makes approximately 600ml
300ml milk
200ml single cream
120g caster sugar
2 vanilla pods, split in half lengthways
7 egg yolks

❋ Place the milk, cream and half the caster sugar in a medium saucepan set over low to medium heat. Add the vanilla pods and bring the mixture to a simmer, stirring occasionally. Remove from the heat and set aside to infuse for 10–15 minutes.

❋ Meanwhile, get ready a clean, large bowl with a sieve set in it.

✳ Beat the egg yolks lightly in another large bowl. Add the remaining sugar and beat well until the mixture is light and fluffy.

✳ Return the pan containing the milk mixture to a high heat and bring to the boil, stirring often. When it rises up the pan, pour it slowly onto the egg yolk mixture, stirring constantly. Then pour the combined mixture through the sieve into the clean bowl. The heat of the milk should have cooked the egg yolks to the required degree.

✳ If not, and the custard is still thin and runny, return the custard to the pan and stir it over a very low heat until it will thickly coat the back of a spoon.

✳ Alternatively, pulse the bowl of custard in the microwave for 30 seconds, retest and repeat until the custard is thickened. Then, pour through another clean sieve into a clean, cold bowl.

✳ As the custard cools, stir it occasionally to prevent a skin from forming. When it is fully cold, chill the custard before serving.

· ·

FLAVOURS AND FILLINGS

CHOCOLATE

 How does a bean become a bar?

Chocolate comes from the cacao, or cocoa bean, which is in fact the seed of a small tree that is native to the Central American tropics. Somewhat appropriately, the name of the tree – *Theobroma cacao* – means 'food of the gods' in Greek.

After the white-pink flowers of the cacao tree are pollinated, some develop into fruits, in the form of large pods 15–30cm long containing several dozen seeds or beans. Once ripe, the pods are collected and split open. Before the beans can be used to make chocolate (or cocoa powder), they have to be fermented by exposure to the sun. After the beans are processed in this way, they are dried and then shipped for roasting, grinding and manufacture.

The cocoa bean is the source of three main products: cocoa butter, cocoa powder and chocolate. Chocolate and cocoa powder feature in many types of baking, while cocoa butter is primarily used in food manufacture and cosmetics.

How was chocolate discovered?

The seeds of the cacao tree, from which chocolate is made, have been used for thousands of years in Central America, where many successive cultures valued their stimulant properties. Seeds, or beans, have been found in ancient sites in Mexico, where the Mayan and later Aztec civilisations revered the tree and believed it had magical and divine properties.

The Mayans and Aztecs did not eat chocolate, though; they drank it. Whole beans were dried and roasted, then ground to a paste and mixed with cold water until a foam appeared. This made quite a bitter drink, which was flavoured with spices including chilli and vanilla and sweetened with honey gathered from tropical bees.

 ## When did chocolate come to Europe?

The explorer Christopher Columbus was the first European to see cacao beans, but it was the Conquistador Hernando Cortés who first tasted the rich, frothy drink made from the beans.

Moctezuma II, the Aztec emperor, welcomed the Spanish in 1519, little knowing what was to come: his new friends ravaged the Aztec empire with measles and stole their gold, before returning to Europe with the cacao beans. News of Aztec gold, as well as chocolate, soon spread throughout Europe's capital cities but the new drink did not take off quickly and it was only when it began to be sweetened with sugar that it became popular throughout Spain. From there the taste for sweetened chocolate spread to France and then to Britain – the first chocolate house opened in London in 1657 followed by other fashionable houses where the wealthy met and drank a variety of chocolate beverages, some of them fairly bitter.

The chocolate drank in those days, however, was very different to the drink we serve today. Until the nineteenth century, the whole cacao bean was used to make the drink, which means that it was probably rather greasy. When the Dutch confectioner Coenraad Johannes van Houton developed a press capable of separating cocoa butter out of the cocoa mass (see page 205 for more on cocoa mass), he produced a dry cocoa powder which was used to make a refined hot chocolate.

The first solid dark chocolate bar was moulded at the J. S. Fry & Sons factory in Bristol in 1847. In 1876, Daniel Peter, a Swiss confectioner, developed the first milk chocolate by adding dried milk powder to the chocolate mass. Not long after, a machine that was capable of grinding the mass much more finely was developed by the Swiss company Lindt, and so chocolate finally began to take shape.

 Do all types of chocolate taste the same?

Not at all! Like wine, chocolate has an amazing range and complexity of flavours and many factors come into play in influencing the taste of a chocolate.

There are three main cultivated varieties of chocolate bean, but the majority of the trees grown today are of the Forastero type. This produces a dark and relatively plain chocolate that you would instantly recognise as it is used to make popular high-street brands. The lesser-grown varieties, which are used in more expensive chocolate, are Criollo and Trinitario (a hybrid of the Forastero and Criollo) and these have a greater range of flavour notes, including fruity and acidic.

Chocolate's flavour will vary according to the type of cacao bean used, but further differences in flavour are created by other factors: the bean's region of origin, its growing conditions and whether the bean has been blended with others all affect the flavour.

Although at first the differences between types of choclate may seem too subtle to appreciate, with time and practice you should be able to pick up on the different 'notes', which make up a chocolate's flavour.

 ## What do the percentages of cocoa solids on chocolate mean for bakers?

The list of ingredients that appears on the back of a chocolate bar wrapper will usually give the percentage of cocoa solids or cocoa mass (sometimes called liquor). Really good-quality chocolate or chocolate made for cooking will advertise the percentage of cocoa solids in large type on the front of the wrapper.

Encouraged by food programmes and other media, we have recently been drawn towards simpler, purer foods, with fewer additives. Chocolate has not been immune to this, and there has been a move to increase the percentage of cocoa mass in chocolate bars and reduce the sugar content. Yet, for baking, it isn't just about a higher cocoa percentage. A balance must be struck between cocoa content and flavour, which is arguably released more fully in the presence of some sugar. The higher the percentage of cocoa solids, the lower the percentage of sugar and so the more bitter or bittersweet the chocolate will be. Certainly chocolate that is 100 per cent cocoa solids is far too bitter to eat – it's best used only for recipes that call for that very strong flavour, for example, in northern Italy, where it is commonly used to enrich game dishes.

There are legal definitions of the different types of chocolate, based on the percentage of cocoa solids, cocoa butter and sugar they contain:

Dark chocolate	at least 35 per cent cocoa solids
Milk chocolate	as little as 20 per cent cocoa solids in the UK, but 25 per cent in Europe
White chocolate	20 per cent cocoa butter (usually processed to remove its strong flavour) and at least 50 per cent sugar

Are chocolates with different percentages interchangeable in baking?

Cocoa solids, cocoa butter and sugar percentages all affect the outcome and taste of a bake.

The more cocoa solids the stronger the taste of chocolate and the more bitter the flavour, which will affect the flavour of your bake in the same way. Similarly, if the cocoa solid percentage you use is too low (less than 40 per cent) the flavour will not be strong or chocolatey enough; too much (over 70 per cent) and the taste may be overwhelming. In many cases, it's just a case of personal preference.

The percentage of sugar that a chocolate contains also affects the way in which the chocolate works in a recipe. The chocolate with the lower cocoa solids has to make up the loss in weight with extra sugar and fat, so your bake may be sweeter than if you had used a chocolate with 70 per cent cocoa solids. But many cooks also find that chocolate with a lower cocoa percentage (and higher sugar percentage) will mix more easily and create a looser mixture when incorporated with other ingredients. If you want to substitute one type of chocolate for another you may find that you also need to adapt the sugar quantity accordingly.

What is cocoa powder and how is it made?

The process of making cocoa powder involves removing most of the fat – the cocoa butter – from the bean after it has been roasted. The beans, or pieces of the bean called nibs, are crushed and pressed. The crushing process squeezes the cocoa butter from the cocoa mass (also known as cocoa solids or liquor). The remaining solidified cocoa mass is then cooled, pulverized and sifted to produce the fine powder with which we are familiar.

Is cocoa powder gluten free?

It should be, but often it's not. This is because while the cacao bean itself does not contain any wheat or gluten, cocoa powder can be manufactured in factories that also process flour or baked goods that contain gluten. Check the small print on the packaging carefully to be sure.

What is the difference between cocoa powder and drinking chocolate and can I bake with both?

Cocoa powder is the pure, ground extract of the cacao bean with most of the cocoa butter removed. Drinking chocolate, while based on cocoa powder, also contains sugar as well as flavourings, emulsifiers and sometimes milk powders. These enable it to be made into a drink more quickly than with plain cocoa, but they mean it's not suitable for baking.

 ## Can I use cocoa powder as a replacement for flour in chocolate sponge recipes?

Cocoa powder is the most highly concentrated source of chocolate flavour, which is why it is so useful in the kitchen, especially for recipes where additional fat is not required or wanted.

Cocoa powder can replace flour in certain cases but only in small quantities (2–3 tablespoons) as cocoa is much drier and harsher in taste than flour and lacks gluten (so the mixture will rely on the eggs to set it) – you may have to adjust the liquid and sugar too. It is usually easier to replace flour with a combination of cocoa and ground nuts in larger sponges.

FLOURLESS CHOCOLATE ROULADE

This recipe uses a simple whisked mixture of eggs and sugar combined with cocoa powder to make a very light sponge. The mixture is very delicate and best suited to making sheets of sponge or thin cakes, which can then be sandwiched with cream and covered in chocolate.

You'll need 350ml whipped double cream to make a roulade with the sponge sheet, or 250ml to sandwich two round sponges.

Makes one sponge sheet or 2 round sponge layers
9 medium eggs at room temperature
2 tablespoons hot water
250g caster sugar
75g cocoa powder

1 baking tray or Swiss roll tin 30 x 40cm, or 2 x 25cm round cake tins or sandwich tins, greased with butter and lined with baking paper

❄ Preheat the oven to 200°C/400°F/gas 6.

❄ Place the eggs and hot water in the bowl of a large free-standing electric mixer and beat lightly together. Add the sugar and whisk for about 10 minutes until the mixture is thick and mousse-like and the whisk leaves a ribbon-like trail when lifted.

❄ While the eggs are being whisked, sift the cocoa powder two or three times through a very fine sieve. Then tip the cocoa into the eggs and fold in using either a large balloon whisk or metal spoon, ensuring that the cocoa is thoroughly incorporated.

❄ Transfer the mixture to the tin(s), gently easing it into an even layer using the back of a spoon or spatula, and place in the oven. Bake for 10–12 minutes until the sponge is cooked and firm to the touch. Remove from the oven and set on a wire rack to cool for 10 minutes before removing from the tin.

Note: If you don't have a large electric mixer, whisk the egg, water and sugar in a heatproof bowl set over another bowl of hot water, or a pan of very gently simmering water (the base of the bowl should not touch the water).

••

 ## Why does my roulade crack when I roll it?

Roulades have a tendency to crack so it's nothing to be ashamed of! If you have a roulade that does crack when you roll it up, it may be that the sponge is too thick. A thinner layer will be less likely to crack, so try baking the sponge in a slightly larger tin.

Overcooking the mixture or using too hot an oven will cause the mixture to become too dry so it will tend to crack. One way you can try to prevent this is to cover the baked sponge with a clean, slightly damp, tea towel to keep the sponge moist as it cools and use an oven thermometer to make sure your oven is at the correct temperature.

Incidentally, roulades are of course not the same thing as a Swiss roll type of whisked sponge, which doesn't usually crack.

How is white chocolate made?

White chocolate is made from essentially the same ingredients as other chocolates, but it does not contain any cocoa solids, which gives other types of chocolate their colour, flavour and texture. As such, white chocolate is creamier and more fat-rich, as it contains a larger proportion of cocoa butter and milk than plain and milk chocolates. The flavour of white chocolate comes from added vanilla – and the milk itself, of course, which lends a noticeable dairy taste.

 ## Can white chocolate be used in baking?

White chocolate can be used in baking, but its flavour is easily masked by other ingredients, so it is best added as chunks, as you might include in muffins or cookies. It can also blend well with fruits such as raspberries and mango, and even mint – flavours that balance out the sweet richness of the white chocolate.

White chocolate can be more difficult to handle because it melts at a lower temperature than milk or dark and it can overcook and stiffen if it gets too warm. Best, then, to break the white chocolate into small pieces and melt it in a glass bowl stood over a pan of hot, but not simmering or boiling water. Alternatively, you can melt it gently on a low setting in the microwave – simply pulse the power in 15-second blasts, stirring the chocolate in between to allow it to melt evenly.

What are chocolate-flavoured cake coverings made from?

Chocolate cake coverings are manufactured from vegetable and dairy fat mixtures that are emulsified, flavoured and sweetened to resemble chocolate. They are used commercially in the production of cheap desserts and confectionery, but they can lack the crisp texture and clear flavour of real chocolate and are often waxy or oily and sweet.

 ## Why does chocolate sometimes develop a white powder on the surface?

The white bloom that you might see on the surface of a chocolate bar is in fact made up from cocoa butter crystals, and it's perfectly safe to eat. This tends to occur when chocolate is kept at too warm a temperature – you will often see it appear on the surface of chocolate that has been melted and allowed to set again. Best, then, to keep your chocolate at a steady cool room temperature, and to eat it as soon as you can after buying, although preferably not before you have baked your chosen dessert!

Chocolate will deteriorate naturally as it ages. As chocolate bars are relatively dry, bacterial or fungal attack is rare, but the aroma, texture and flavour of the chocolate will suffer long before it actually goes off. If it's kept cool and dry, it should keep for many years, but it will eventually lose so much of its taste that it will be unpleasant. To be sure you are using only chocolate at its very best, always check the 'best before' date.

 ## What is couverture?

Chocolates sold for use in cooking, baking and pastry work are usually labelled with both the total percentage of cocoa and the word 'couverture' or the percentage of cocoa butter.

Couverture (from the French word meaning 'coating') is a term used by chocolatiers to denote a chocolate that is made with between 32 and 39 per cent cocoa butter. The higher the cocoa butter content, the more liquid and pliable the chocolate will be when melted, and the easier it will be to mould into thin sheets for covering a dessert or mixing with other ingredients.

 ## What is the best way to melt chocolate?

Gently and slowly – you should never rush chocolate. It is best done in a heatproof bowl set over a pan of warm, body-temperature water (37°C/99°F), no hotter. Take care not to let any of the water, or steam from it, come into contact with the chocolate or it may 'seize' (see page 216). Remove from the heat when the chocolate has softened sufficiently and stir it until it is smooth. You can also use a microwave set on a medium heat in short pulses of 15 seconds, stirring the chocolate in between each pulse. White chocolate, incidentally, will melt at a lower temperature than dark chocolate so needs to be watched even more carefully.

If you are melting chocolate together with butter, cream or another fatty ingredient, you can do this in a pan directly over a very gentle heat. Take care not to allow the mixture to heat above 40°C/104°F because the chocolate can easily be overheated and turn grainy.

 How is chocolate tempered?

When couverture chocolate (see page 213) is manufactured, the cocoa butter is blended and cooled before being heated and cooled again at closely controlled temperatures, which gives the chocolate a texture that snaps when you break it. If chocolate is not tempered when it is melted, the crystals of cocoa butter will form in random, unstable sizes and will not give the crisp, glossy finish that confectioners look for.

Careful melting, reheating and then cooling of the chocolate again at precise temperatures stabilises the crystals and gives a shiny finish. You can do this at home, but you will need a sugar thermometer.

❋ Place chopped chocolate into a large mixing bowl and heat gently, either over a pan of warm water or in a microwave until it melts and reaches 50°C/122°F (45°C/113°F for white chocolate).

 Pour most of the chocolate into a clean bowl and stir it until it cools to 26°C, then return the chocolate to the original bowl and heat to 32°C/89.6°F (28°C/82.4°F for white chocolate), before cooling again.

It is also possible to very gently melt chocolate so that its temperature reaches 31°C/87.8°F but does not exceed 32°C/89.6°F. Within this range, unstable crystals of cocoa butter will melt and, when the mixture cools, will be transformed into stable crystals. As you can imagine, this is difficult to do at home without the strict temperature control of a tempering machine, although small versions are available for the home baker.

Why does chocolate sometimes go oily and stiff when heated?

Chocolate will go hard and 'seize' for several reasons. The usual cause is that water has crept into it: the smallest amount, even steam, can cause the cocoa solids and cocoa butter to split out of emulsion with one another. The chocolate loses its liquid sheen and turns into a stiff, oily, grainy mass. At a high temperature, the cocoa butter will remain liquid and oily, and the cocoa mass will eventually clump into a hard lump.

It is distressing to see this happen when you are carefully melting chocolate for your dessert, but it's sometimes possible to reverse this process by adding a small quantity of butter, melting it and stirring it through the mixture. This will hopefully bring the chocolate back into its former smoothness, although it will no longer be suitable for fine work. You can, however, incorporate it into another recipe, particularly one that contains a large amount of fat or liquid. Brownies would be a good choice, or a chocolate sauce.

 ## What is ganache?

Ganache is a mixture of chocolate and cream that's used to make chocolate truffles or as a topping and filling for gâteaux. Ganache mixtures can also contain butter, which gives them a thicker, more luxurious texture.

You can make a simple ganache either by melting chocolate and folding it into whipped cream (this is not for the faint-hearted as the chocolate will begin to set instantly), or by melting chocolate in hot cream before cooling and then whipping to incorporate air. The key to success with this second method is not to overheat the chocolate in the cream. Chop the chocolate finely so that it will melt quickly, then add it to warm cream off the heat and allow the chocolate to melt slowly without overworking the cream by beating too hard, which may cause the chocolate to seize.

Because of its acidity, chocolate made from Criollo beans (see page 204) can split or curdle hot cream, causing the liquids to separate from the solids. So if you are making ganache with Criollo chocolate, take care not to heat the cream above body temperature.

For a ganache that is soft at room temperature, mix chocolate and cream in proportions of 1:1 (e.g. 100g of chocolate to 100ml cream). This consistency makes a lovely coating for a cream and berry-filled chocolate sponge.

For a firmer ganache, which will be more stable, use a higher proportion of chocolate, in a ratio up to 2:1. Use this for desserts such as brownies or to make simple truffles rolled in crushed ginger biscuits.

FLAVOURS AND FILLINGS

INDEX

INDEX

ALSO AVAILABLE FROM
THE GREAT BRITISH
BAKE OFF

How to achieve baking perfection at home, with foolproof recipes and simple step-by-step masterclasses based on Mary and Paul's Technical Challenges.

Easy recipes for sharing with your family, or for learning new techniques and skills to create delicious treats.

Baking doesn't have to be complicated to be 'showstopping'. Inspired by the Showstopper Challenge, here are bakes that will both turn heads and make mouths water.

WWW.BAKEOFFBOOK.CO.UK

Recipes from your favourite show, now in your pocket! Download The Great British Bake Off app and get 50 amazing recipes.